Salvador Mafé Huertas

Eurofighter Typhoon

Dedicated to my brothers Tomás, Jorge, Fernando and Pepe, thanks for being there.

KAGERO

MORE FROM KAGERO

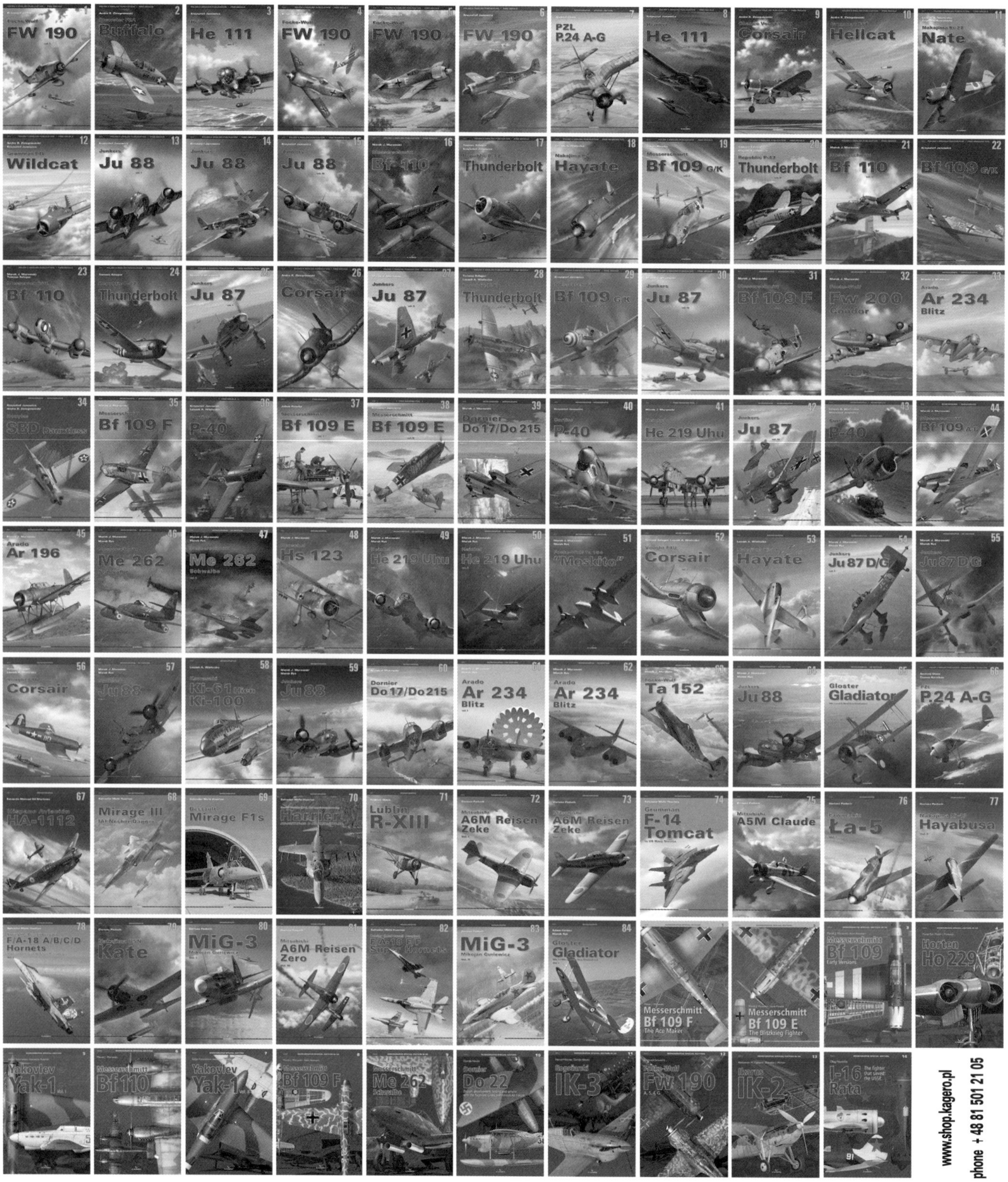

Eurofighter Typhoon • Salvador Mafé Huertas • First edition • LUBLIN 2022

 • Printed in Poland/Wydrukowano w Polsce • **ISBN 978-83-66673-98-4**

Color profiles: **Arkadiusz Wróbel** • Photos: **Ejército del Aire, Eurofighter, Airbus Military, Jorge Portalés, Manuel Acosta, Tono Fernández, Rafael Treviño, Luftwaffe, NATO Aircom, S. Mafé** • Cover photo credit: **Manuel Acosta Zapata** • DTP: KAGERO STUDIO – Łukasz Maj

KAGERO Publishing
Akacjowa 100, Turka, os. Borek, 20-258 Lublin 62, Poland, phone/fax: (+48) 81 501 21 05
www.kagero.pl • e-mail: kagero@kagero.pl, marketing@kagero.pl, shop@kagero.pl
w w w . k a g e r o . p l
Distribution: **KAGERO Publishing**

Beautiful image of a Group 11 driver, about to undertake a night training mission. [JM Martínez Álvarez]

The Eurofighter program is the most important military and industrial collaboration project that has ever been carried out in the Old Continent. Originally born as an air superiority fighter, intended to counteract the numerical superiority of the Warsaw Pact air forces, after the end of the Cold War it has gradually become a true multi-purpose fighter, possibly the most advanced that exists nowadays, with the possible exception of the North American F-35 Lightning II. It is true that its entry into service was extended over time, there were many new technologies applied in which the European companies involved in its development had to start from scratch: electronic equipment, pilot equipment, etc. But this has been, within its difficulty, the least problematic. The really difficult thing has been that the four partners agreed to go overcoming the milestones that the program was presenting as the months and years passed. Spain has always shown itself to be a very reliable partner and its industry, led by EADS-CASA (now Airbus Defense & Space), has been able to respond effectively and decisively to the challenges that continually presented themselves. We can not say the same of Germany, where the Eurofighter issue became an internal domestic political argument, with ongoing debates in the Federal Parliament, but today these debates have already been largely overcome, although its operational availability rate is the most low of all users.

Since the Air Force received its first Typhoon of series CE.16-01 / 11-70 (11-01), until the reception of the last of the initial purchase, the C.16-78, during this spring, these years they have supposed a new revolution of modernity, as in its day it supposed the incorporation of the F-18 Hornet, but perhaps of greater importance. Keep in mind that from the beginning you have all the information about your ability to make improvements and updates, in addition to exercising control over all equipment and systems, along with other European air forces associated. This is something unusual and that does not happen when you buy American material. With the Eurofighter Typhoon, the full capacity of the system is available from the beginning, without any restrictions.

Salvador Mafé Huertas

Introduction

How is the Eurofighter: design, construction and features

The operational requirements for the Eurofighter Typhoon, currently considered the most advanced fighter aircraft on the current scene along with the F-22 and

F-35, were agreed upon by the Chiefs of Air Staff of Germany, Spain, England and Italy, in the form of a document called European Staff

A Typhoon Tranche 1 of Group 11 flying over Utrera. [Wing 11]

Pilot of the 111 Squadron on board of one of the Eurofighters deployed in the Vilkas detachment. [C. Schrik]

Requirement in 1985, whose validity would be reconfirmed in 1994.

This agreement formed the basis of the project for the development of an extremely agile aircraft, destined to dominate the skies of the first half of the 21st century. This should be a twin-engine and single-seater, with optimal performance in the combat beyond the visual range and in close combat and also have a significant ground attack capacity. This duality of missions has been a reality for a few years, so that the aircraft can take off with a mixed load of air-to-air and air-ground weapons and after take-off it can modify its objectives according to needs, or once the mission to attack targets on land, if fuel permits, change to an air superiority

Among the different DASS equipment in the right pod is the towed radar DECOY (TRD: Towed Radar Decoy). [S. Mafé]

The Eurofighter F-2000A of the 4th Stormo of the AMI with the mark of the 100,000 flight hours of the fleet. [Eurofighter]

intervention. It is what is called "swing role", the change of mission.

Its main dedication was to be that of air defense, for which modern doctrines are conceived by proposing interception beyond the visual range of the pilot. In these circumstances, the interceptor must detect the aircraft that constitutes the threat at a great distance, accelerate at supersonic speed, launch its BVRAAM or SRAAM weaponry and quickly break to avoid the response in the form of another missile fired by the adversary.

The typical intervention would begin with the detection of a target more than 130 km away. Next, the Eurofighter Typhoon accelerates to Mach 1.8 to approach its target and so that the guided missile achieves as much kinetic energy as possible. Once fired, the aircraft breaks its flight path, aided by its great maneuverability at high speed and the DASS self-defense system, to avoid the opponent's response that can take the form of another similar missile.

The crystallization of these requirements is a stylized single-seater with a low-hanging delta wing, which presents the innovation of having front canard planes.

The latest generations of European combat aircraft, the Swedish Gripen and the French Rafale, in addition to the Eurofighter Typhoon, have favored the choice of canard configurations. These surfaces are destabilizing, in contrast to the stabilizing function of the tailplanes. In exchange for a modest reduction of performance in subsonic regime, the canard planes present a great advantage in supersonic maneuverability.

To achieve air superiority both in air defense missions and in closed combat and also the quality of not requiring fields that are too long, a high

Typhoon FGR4 of the RAF making a climb to full afterburning. [Crown Copyright / MOD]

thrust / weight ratio and a low wing load are required (aircraft weight divided by area) of the wing. The high maneuverability in closed combat requires at the same time an efficient aerodynamic configuration, capable of providing a high lift / drag ratio and a high lift available.

The high maneuverability is favored in an aircraft that is "controlled unstable" and this depends on the relative position between the center of aerodynamic pressures of the aircraft and the center of gravity. The further apart they are, the more unstable the configuration. In the Eurofighter the position of the CdG is very backward, which in combination with the planes canard, gets a naturally unstable aircraft, so it is essential to use fly by wire to fly it.

The presence of canard planes provides other advantages, for example during landing, since they can be deflected to act as airbrakes from the moment the plane touches the ground. The clean lines at the back of the plane, with a minimum cross section, no rear aerodynamic brakes, or thrust reversers that they hinder, as in the Tornado, they lead to a favorable distribution of the

EF-2000 of the Luftwaffe deployed in the Baltic Air Policing landing on the runway of the Amari Air Base, Estonia. [Luftwaffe]

A Typhoon of the RAF in the engine test bench, with the EJ200 at full power. [Eurojet]

As a complement to the single-seater basic version, a two-seater variant has been developed. This externally conserves the same dimensions. Its mission is mainly that of assuming the functions of pilot trainer, and for the training of weapons, nevertheless it conserves the capacity of complete combat. This version is fully operable from the front seat. [S. Mafé]

area, which translates positively in the generation of a resistance of reduced wave in supersonic regime, for such a short plane.

With a thrust / weight ratio that exceeds 1.2, the Eurofighter can take off in 300 meters and climb vertically once the wheels have left the ground. Landing is something else. The maximum distance needed to stop the aircraft is 700 meters using aerodynamic braking, wheel braking and deployment of the 4 m braking parachute. in diameter, which is housed in the base of the vertical drift, as usual. This represents the worst case, with the wet track and crosswind.

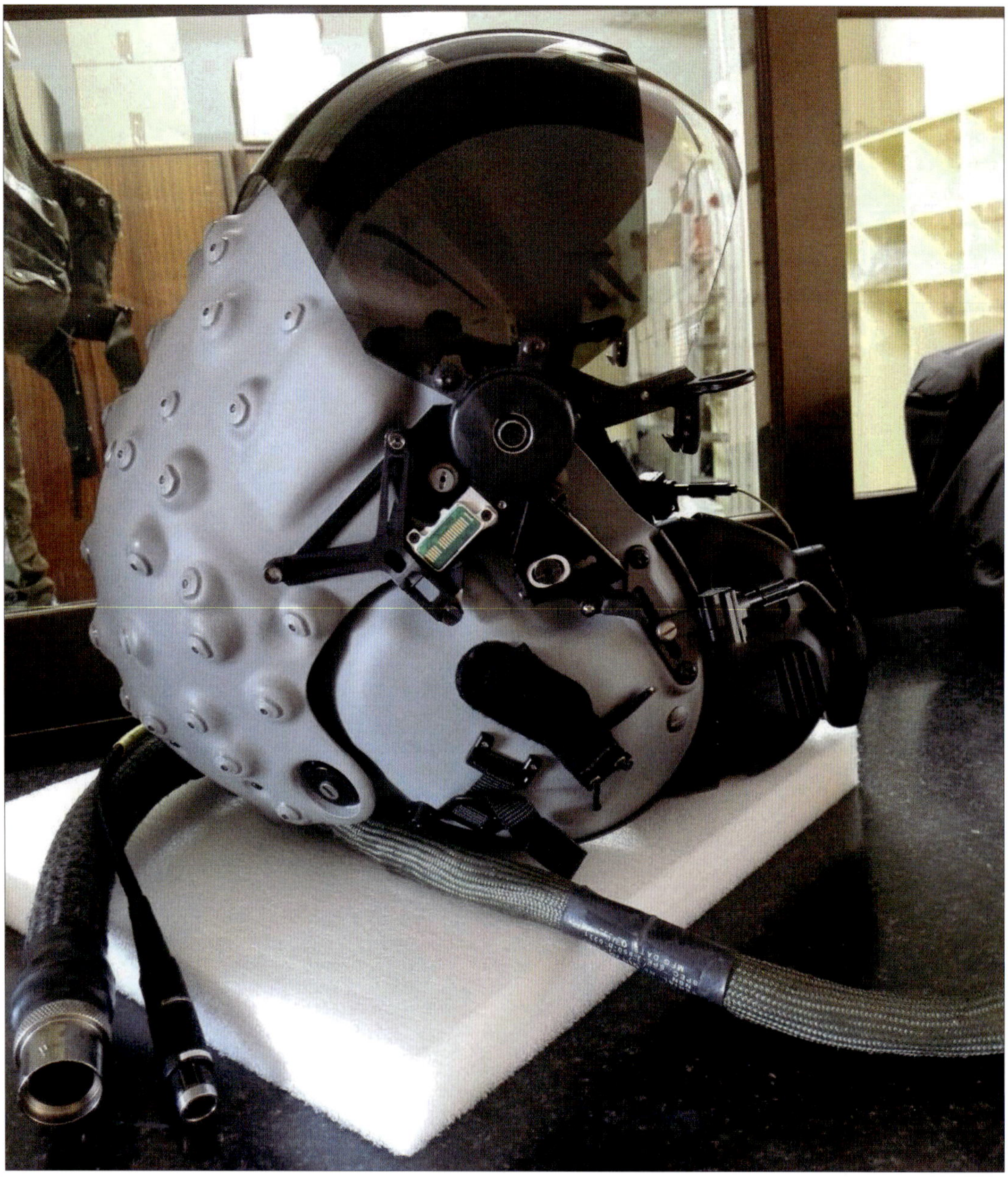

The electronic helmet called HMSS, has many functions, but has no night vision capability, so BAE is in the final stages of development of the Striker 2 that does, but it is unknown if the Air Force will adopt; Meanwhile the Gentex ACS Helmet helmet with Anvis night vision goggles is used. [S. Mafé]

Under normal conditions the landing race must be shorter.

In summary, the design of the airplane is very clean aerodynamically speaking and that translates into speed, hence its ease to fly in a supercruise.

The aerodynamic drag generated at supersonic speed by such a large wing is minimized by the arrow of its leading edge which is 53 ° and a low value of the thickness / rope ratio, which is approximately 4%. The subsonic lift is improved by the use of the leading edge slats.

The high structural strength and rigidity / weight ratio of the Eurofighter has been achieved by the use of a combination of composite materials, conventional metals and special alloys, in combination with a new construction system.

An innovative feature of the Eurofighter is that, structurally speaking, the "skin" of the fuselage absorbs a larger part of structural loads compared to the designs of previous generations.

It emphasizes the intensive use of composite materials, in which the compounds in carbon and glass are used as resistant fibers. The use of compounds reaches 60% by weight (55% Carbon Fiber and 5% Fiberglass) in 75% of the total exposed area, including the fuselage, wings, flaperons and vertical drift. The wings, with the exception of the anchor fittings with the fuselage and some other connection element, are constructed with carbon-based composite material, including the internal spars, which are glued during the autoclave curing process, and the two skins , which are integral. The fibers used are of new generation and are agglutinated to form panels or pieces with a resin, of the family of Bismaldeimides, which acts as an adhesive. The advantage it presents over epoxy is its greater resistance to temperature; while the epoxy collapses around 215° C, the others raise that limit to 400°. The drawback is its high price.

The "office" of the Eurofighter pilot is wide, comfortable (within limits), well organized and ergonomic; As the saying goes, it was designed by pilots for pilots, which is very true. [S.Mafé]

The "office" of the Eurofighter pilot is wide, comfortable (within limits), well organized and ergonomic; As the saying goes, it was designed by pilots for pilots, which is very true. [S.Mafé]

The "office" of the Eurofighter pilot is wide, comfortable (within limits), well organized and ergonomic; As the saying goes, it was designed by pilots for pilots, which is very true. [S.Mafé]

The Eurofighter Typhoon Head-Up Display is a state-of-the-art model. [S.Mafé]

Its use is one of the causes of the low weight of the aircraft in relation to its size and is estimated at a saving of 30% compared to a structure entirely built in metal. This saving is obtained in the construction of individual pieces, while for the calculation of the complete structure it would be reduced a little, reaching 20%.

As for the metallic materials, aluminum-lithium plates are used as raw material for the conformation of the leading edges of the wing, the vertical drift and the ailerons. Where the obtaining of pieces by casting is needed, the most conventional aluminum alloys are preferred. Exceptions include the cockpit floor, the pilot's footrest and the avionics compartment roof, which are formed by superplastic stamping of lithium-aluminum alloy material. Ti50 (Titanium) is also used. The metallic content reaches 10% in titanium and 25% for the aluminum-lithium alloys and 5% of conventional aeronautical aluminum.

The metal is preferably used in frontal areas where there is a risk of impacts with birds and which are normally relatively thin and highly demanded in case of impact. An exception is made to the radome of the radar and the upper careening of the vertical drift that need to be "transparent" to the radar radiations, as well as the cockpit, for obvious reasons of visibility.

The power plant chosen for the Eurofighter consists of two EJ200 turbofan engines, which is the latest and most powerful representative of European technology. [Eurojet]

The specifications of the Eurofighter require a resistance to the impact of a bird of 1 kg. (2.2 pounds) of weight at a speed of 887 km/h (480 knots).

Initially it was foreseen that the construction of the front planes would be from composite materials, but finally they were constructed of titanium, using the new technique of superplastic forming and gluing by diffusion. The ailerons (wing flaperones) are constructed in a similar way.

The wing of the Eurofighter is multilongueron, glued to the lower skin at the time of manufacture. This set is equipped with pipes, train anchors and other internal elements and then closed with the upper skin. The responsibility for the construction of the right wing comp The responsibility for the construction of the full right wing and the slats of both wings, is from EADS CASA (Airbus Defence & Space), which delivers them ready to install. The design of the wing - and in general of the whole airplane - was made using advanced electronic models in 3D, by means of the CAD/CAM CATIA system.

The structure is reinforced to withstand + 9 / -3g usable with a realistic combat mass, ie with weapons and full internal fuel load. However, in these conditions the pilot will be helped by the contribution of the SCV (Flight Control System) with its "Careless Driving" mode, in such a way that it will allow maximum performance and never exceed the structural limits. .

The use of composite materials allows a quick repair of the damages suffered in combat and considerable efforts have been made to develop these techniques.

Both versions, the single-seater and the two-seater, use a dorsal aerodynamic brake, which is not very usual as it usually tends to avoid placing

The factors that contribute to the excellent performance of the EJ200 are the use of large rope aerofoils for the single-crystal titanium blades in the five stages of the compressor. The blades are equipped with a sophisticated multi-pass internal cooling system. The use of compressor and low weight turbine assemblies is possible thanks to the use of highly effective integral blade discs and "brush" joints, finally backed by adequate margins of behavior in the face of airflow situations. Irregular (emerges), using a single step of fixed air guide spans for the compressor and a high-performance afterburner system derived from the separate fuel burn, both in the cold flow from the initial bypass from the fan, of the hot coming from the power turbine. [S. Mafé]

The display pilot of Group 11 demonstrating the capabilities of the Eurofighter. [Sergio Ruiz González]

them aligned with the vertical drift or tail planes to avoid the negative effect on them of the turbulence generated at the unfold it Other examples that use a dorsal brake like the F-15, F/A-18 and the Russian Sukhoi have two vertical drifts, with which the turbulence passes between them. However, the breach of this rule seems to work well in the Eurofighter Typhoon, since it has previous experience of the EAP * whose tests were satisfactory and that have been corroborated with the direct experience of the aircraft.

The last external element worthy of mention are the two fixed lateral fins placed on the sides of the cabin. Its function is to order the air flow at large angles of attack and minimize the directional destabilizing effect (yaw) due to the vertical drift fanning due to the generated turbulence.

The main landing gear, although it is implanted in the wings, folds inward in the fuselage, in this way it is allowed to keep the section of the wing thin and free space to locate weapon supports.

* The EAP (Experimental Aircraft Program) was a demonstration technology aircraft developed as a private project of the British company British Aerospace in the 1980s and which was finally established as the basis for the development of the European multi-purpose fighter Eurofighter Typhoon.

The two-seater

As a complement to the basic single-seater version, a two-seater variant has been developed. This externally conserves the same dimensions. Its mission is mainly to assume the functions of pilot trainer and weapons training, however it retains full combat capability. This version is fully operable from the front seat.

The location of a second cockpit behind the first one has needed to occupy the space used for the avionics hold in the car, which has been located in the space originally reserved for fuel transfer tank No. 1. A certain volume of internal fuel has It has also been sacrificed, although it has been partly offset by a fuel tank located in the rear cowl of the cabin. The rear cockpit is similar to the front and has ejection control, so that the rear cockpit is uncoupled from the first and the plane can be operated from there completely.

In comparison with the car, it suffers a minimum reduction of the radius of action and the time of permanence in the air combat patrols due to the additional weight and the reduction of the internal content of fuel. In this aspect we must bear in mind that there is always the possibility of refueling in flight. The punctual benefits remain practically unchanged.

The use of the two-seater depends on the evolution of the requirements of each air force, but it is clear that it is the most suitable to perform certain tasks in which the use of attack weapons is very demanding in procedures and therefore would produce a high workload for the pilot of the car (for example the maritime attack, the recognition and the designation of low-level targets, etc).

The ejection seat

For any fighter pilot the ejection seat of his aircraft is a vital component, although he hopes never to use it.

The Eurofighter Typhoon emergency escape system is constituted by the Martin Baker Mk16A ejection seat in the 0-0 category, which has the reputation of being one of the most sophisticated in the world. Like the same aircraft, it is built with light alloys and advanced composite materials and has many advantages over previous designs. Ergonomics and maintainability have received a high priority during conception in order to maximize safety and minimize the workload of maintenance personnel. The drastic reduction of weight demanded has been achieved in the design of the two cylindrical tubes that constitute the propulsion system so that they have a double function: to act as main structural elements assuming all the ejection loads, in flight and impact.

t is directly derived from the Martin Baker Mk15, the lightest and smallest of the seats currently in production, which was designed to meet the needs of the market of high performance turboprop trainers.

Reliability and maintainability are key elements of a design that facilitates full access to its components when installed in the cockpit. The seat offers a high level of comfort and is integrated with the MSOGS (Molecular Sieve Oxygen Generation System) onboard system, the anti-g, the NBQ defense and communications system, together with interfaces for the helmet-mounted systems . The reduced size of the headrest contributes to the excellent unobstructed visibility towards the sides and upwards that the pilot enjoys, a condition that is essential for an effective use of the visor system mounted on the helmet.

The workload of the pilot and consequently the stress that suffers in the ejection process, always compromised, has been reduced with the Mk16A. The only thing that the pilot must do to generate the escape sequence is to pull the ejection lever. From that moment on, the entire sequence of events is automatic and computer controlled. From the detachment of the cockpit, until the pilot hangs from his parachute. Once the seat is ejected from the cabin, a rocket motor is ignited to safely separate the aircraft seat, while deploying two stabilizing wings and a braking parachute to level and control it. From this moment, technology enters into action. The sensing devices are activated and the air speed and altitude data are sent to a digital microprocessor or

The hydraulic system is separated into two redundant and independent systems. The operating pressure is 275.6 bar (4,000 psi) and provides the power to move the flight control surfaces (flaperons, canard, rudder, slats, lips of the air intake,) folding and deploying the landing gear and its direction, barrel, opening / closing of the cabin and erection / folding of the refueling probe in flight. [S. Mafé]

electronic sequencer, together with the values of the acceleration that the seat is experiencing. The computer then determines the safest sequence of events to deploy the parachute and separate from the pilot, all in milliseconds.

Flying at 600 knots and at sea level the pilot, in case of being forced to eject, will be hanging from the parachute in 1.8 seconds since he activated the lever. In ejections at low speed and altitude the parachute is deployed at an impressive 0.7 seconds since the lever has been activated.

Test sequences have been made on land at 450 and 600 ejection knots with satisfactory results, both for the front seat and for the rear seat. Operationally it will be usable from 0 to 1,112 km / h (0-600 knots) of speed and from 0 to 18,044 m. (55,000 feet) altitude.

Electrical and hydraulic system

In an aircraft that depends largely on the electrical system, it has been designed to avoid the risk of a total loss of power generation. This has been achieved through a high level of redundancy and partition of the systems. A DC battery supplies the power for APU starts, as well as for making a limited list of services on the ground and in emergencies. Each of the 30 kVA * generators driven by the motors provide alternating current at 115 / 120V and 400 Hz frequency through two transformers / rectifiers. In case of failure of the transformers, two additional generators for the supply of direct current enter the line.

The hydraulic system is separated into two redundant and independent systems. The operating pressure is 275.6 bar (4,000 psi) and they provide the power to move the flight control surfaces (flaperons, canard, rudder, slats, lips of the air intake) folding and unfolding the train of landing and its direction, cannon, opening / closing of the cabin and erection / folding of the refueling probe in flight.

In the event of failure of an engine, both hydraulic systems are energized by the active engine and the primary flight controls are protected against the loss of liquid from the system by individual isolation valves.

* The kVA is a unit of apparent power of an electrical device with mainly inductive characteristics when operating with alternating current, whose equivalence is normally 1 kVA = 0.8 KW. When we have the power in kVA they are giving us the sum between the useful power (kW) and the reactive power, which indicates the consumption or total contribution of power.

The Power Plant

The Eurofighter power plant is composed of two EJ200 turbofan engines, the latest and most powerful representative of European technology. It is specifically designed to meet the performance requirements for the performance of the Eurofighter mission.

The decision to choose this model of motor was preceded by a series of discussions among the members of the consortium, which is worth reviewing. As it is known, in 1985 the European Staff Requirement was issued followed by the Definition of the Project, from what was known at that time as the European Fighter Aircraft (EFA), which was undertaken between September 1985 and September 1986. Opinions encountered began to be felt even in that early phase of the project.

The concern was evident when it became evident that the Eurofighter should be a large aircraft, of the order of 12.5 tons of empty weight, if it had to comply with the requirements of the RAF. The British air force had always preferred a large aircraft, of at least 11 tons of empty weight, in order to have a greater range and an improved air-ground capacity. The drawback of a large aircraft was the difficulty to export it and therefore, it was not favored by the other three members of the consortium. This finally led to England relaxing its parameters, accepting a somewhat smaller plane.

It became clear that the design of a new motor plant suitable for the project, although benefiting from previous experiences, would require time, so in order not to stop the program waiting for that engine, it was decided that the prototypes would start flying with a interim engine waiting for the definitive.

The PIRATE system is located on the left front side of the cockpit. [S. Mafé]

Indeed, three of the consortium members, including Germany, were not only large-scale operators of the Panavia Tornado, but also manufacturers of the same, including the RB199 engines that equipped the aircraft. Therefore, the wide availability of spare parts and infrastructure seemed to recommend the use of this engine to propel the first Eurofighter aircraft. For reasons never explained, Germany proposed the American General Electric F404 engine, not only for the prototypes, but for the series aircraft, possibly moved for reasons of savings in development costs.

In this trance there was the curious paradox that even Spain, the only one of the four countries that actually operated that engine model, agreed to the use of the RB199 for the first 20 examples of the Eurofighter, defending a European option to reduce the dependence of the Americans. This was, after all, one of the premises with which the Eurofighter program was born.

Finally the good sense prevailed, choosing in July of 1989 the version RB199-200, with a thrust of 75,60 kN (17,000 pounds) which supposed about 4,45 kN (1,000 pounds more powerful than the F404-400 installed in the F-20, but somewhat less powerful than the variant F404/RM 12 installed in the Swedish Gripen.

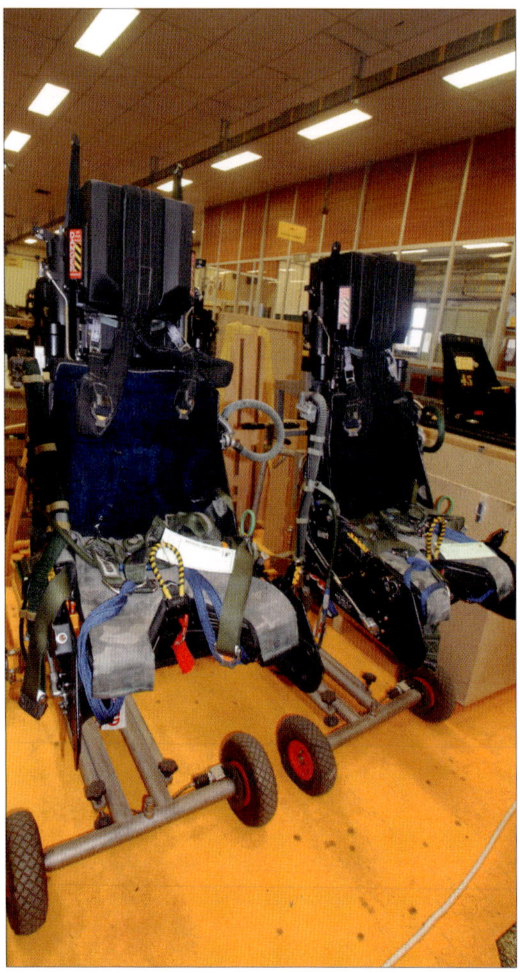

The Eurofighter Typhoon emergency escape system consists of the Martin Baker Mk16A ejection seat in the 0-0 category, which has the reputation of being one of the most sophisticated in the world. Like the same aircraft, it is built with light alloys and advanced composite materials and has many advantages over previous designs, maintenance of the third step is carried out in the Survival Workshop of the Albacete Maintenance Depot. [S. Mafé]

Obviously the anchors of the RB199, the aircraft and the EJ200, were made compatible to facilitate the installation of the latter, once they were available, without complicated structural procedures. This flexibility also provided the possibility of retro-installing the new engine in the Tornado fleet, if necessary.

The delays experienced in the program have allowed the engine, which was only delayed six months according to its initial program, "catch the plane", so the plans to install the RB199 in the first 20 or 30 aircraft were abandoned, allowing to equip all the prototypes with the EJ200 in some of its variants.

Dimensionally the RB199 and the EJ200 are similar (in diameter) and the most notable external differences are the petals of the convergent-divergent exhaust nozzle, which are longer and aerodynamically clean and are optimized to deliver a high thrust with high-temperature post-combustion and high Mach number.

To undertake the design and manufacture of the EJ200, a consortium was formed by the four nations associated and represented by Rolls-Royce (UK), DASA MTU-Munchen GmbH (Germany), FIAT Avio (Italy) and ITP (Spain). The consortium responsible for the motorization was called Eurojet Turbo GmbH.

The new engine owes a lot to the Rolls-Royce technology demonstrator called Advanced Core

Military Engine (ACME) and designated XG40, from the early 80s, although it has incorporated later technological innovations.

The XG40 was launched for the first time on December 23, 1987, generating 88.95 kN (20,000 pounds) of thrust with a thrust/weight ratio of 10:1. This was 40% more than what RB.199 was able to produce, that is why the denomination. At that time it was considered that these benefits were the expression of the maximum that could be achieved in terms of the temperatures of entry into the turbine, for reasons of strength of the materials and what the mixture of kerosene and air could produce.

The EJ200 was launched for the first time on November 28, 1988, achieving the desired thrust only two hours after the start of the trial. The first engine was delivered to MTU for testing, the second to FIAT and the third to Filton. This last engine was later sent to the University of Stuttgart. The engine returned to Bristol to be subjected to the accelerated tests of persistence in simulated mission, being sent later to Pyestcok for the post-combustion tests.

The EJ200 production standard began the flight tests in October 1999 installed in the Italian DA3 prototype. Successively they were installed in the other prototypes.

At that time EJ200 development engines had already accumulated 3,600 hours of tests installed on the seven prototypes, of which 1,170 were flight hours. In December, the first stop and start-up in flight was made. At the end of March 2001, NETMA awarded the Eurojet consortium with the technical certification for the standard production version differentiated by the designation -03Z and this event means the end of the long process of tests in banks and in flight. In June 2001, after a period of paralysis to incorporate updates, the DA2 resumed flight with the brand new EJ-200-3Z, instead of the -3Y, representative of the latest development variant.

The current EJ200 is capable of providing 90 kN (20,250 pounds) of static thrust with afterburning, a dry thrust of 61 kN (13,500 pounds) with a weight of 1,035 kg. (2,284 pounds) that result in a 10: 1 weight-to-weight ratio that equates to the values of the XG40.

Optimized for air-air missions, some of its parameters are:

Compression ratio: 25: 1
Ratio of derivation: 0.4: 1
Temperature peak at the output of the stator: 1,800º K
Length with afterburner: 4.000 mm. (157.4 inches)
Diameter: 990 mm (38.9 inches)

A development program was established, so that by 1998 a representative engine had to be available and that it had to perform more than 10,600 hours of bench tests, during which, naturally supplemented by the tests carried out in flight, the engine was capable to demonstrate a thrust in accordance with the specifications, a generation of operating temperatures and a specific fuel consumption lower than those specified, and a resistance to drowning with adequate and demonstrated full thrust. All this using grids before the admission to simulate a reduced air flow corresponding to the flight with high incidence. Tests of impact resistance with birds were also satisfactory, registering a minimum thrust transition and,

The Eurofighter has a folding ladder for access to the cockpit. [S. Mafé]

In both Group 11 and Wing 14, there are Airbus technicians supporting the respective maintenance squadrons.

The Eurofighter carries the Litening III pod in the central pylon, so its sensors cover almost all angles. [S. Mafé]

finally, a precise and predictable control of the engine, favored by the use of FADEC (Full Authority Digital Engine Control).

The smoke emissions from the leaks not only improved with respect to the original specifications, but the measured emission levels were below the visual threshold.

The start-up is carried out by means of an APU (Auxilary Power Unit) whose exhaust nozzle can be seen near the left wing socket, by the black spot caused by the exhaust gases.

The first EJ200 production standard was delivered on June 1, 2001, to be installed on IPA1. In total, 19 engines were delivered to the four production lines during 2001. In 2002, 34 engines had been delivered and by the end of the same year 188 had been delivered. All the tests in the bank for the certification of the engines that were going to enter service They concluded with a cumulative total of 14,458 test hours of which 5,000 were in the altitude test chamber.

Shortly after, NETMA (NATO Management Agency of Eurofighter and Tornado) declared the engines ready for entry into service and issued the technical certification on March 8, 2001.

Operational engines include improvements such as increased life of the high pressure compressor and low pressure turbine, as well as im-

A Eurofighter of the 14th Wing about to depart on a night mission, it can be seen that it still does not carry the unit numerals. [S. Mafé]

proved cooling of the high pressure turbine. Likewise, a phased program was developed to allow improvements packages to be progressively incorporated. For example, to achieve an improvement of 25% of the useful life for the engines "on the wing", increase the dry thrust to 78 kN (17,539 pounds) and combat power to 120 kN (26,996 pounds) with afterburning.

These features required a new pressure system with a high flow fan, a higher pressure ratio and adaptations to the low pressure turbine.

Some improvements are subject to discussion with customers, whose representative is NETMA, and the main one would be to improve the cost of operation throughout the life cycle, initially stipulated in 6,000 hours of flight (16,000 cycles) and 25 years, as well as the costs of incorporating the new benefits. In this sense, the same priority has been assigned to reliability, maintainability and ease of testing, as well as to the benefits and flight safety throughout the development program. Consequently, special attention has been paid to ensuring that reliability and maintainability are facilitated by the incorporation of a system for monitoring the engine's status and diagnosis, which allows maintenance according to needs and considerably lowers operating costs.

With the EJ200 installed, the Eurofighter can perform the takeoff rotation in less than 300 meters, which is the agreed contract value, and from the release of the brakes until it is flying at an altitude of 11,582 m (38000 ft) to 1 , 5 Mach in two and a half minutes, something very remarkable.

The original order was for 620 aircraft, later reduced by the four partners, as well as the manufacture of not less than 1,500 engines, which have been built in three batches of 363, 519 and 500 corresponding to Tranches 1, 2 and 3.

The future of the EJ200

One of the requirements demanded in the EJ200 was that it had a certain growth potential, as does the Eurofighter. In the case of the EJ200, the motor should have a value of approximately 20%; this potential would develop in successive phases. The truth is that the EuroJet consortium did not stay there, but managed to design an engine with a growth potential of 30%. Now, at present, part of this growth potential is already implanted in the engine, being able to provide some 21,250 pounds of thrust or 95 kN, although this feature is not used, as it would reduce the life of its components.

Therefore, if you wanted to develop the capacity of the engine to reach that extra 30%, it would be necessary to act on key elements of it, the main one being the compressor and the turbine. They planned to undertake two phases, the so-called stage or phase 1 and the stage or phase 2, being in the latter where most of the modifications would be carried out. The life cycle of the program indicated that this would take place in 2016, date in which the Eurofighter would have entered into a hypothetical MLU (Mid Life Upgrade) which, unfortunately, given the economic conditions, was not possible, although it is true that the aircraft of Tranche 3A are already flying. One paragraph: the Tranche 3 incorporates a series of improvements that give the Eurofighter the maximum of its capabilities both electronic and design (conformable tanks), but due to the aforementioned crisis, has been divided into Tranche 3A and Tranche 3B. The Tranche 3A contemplates a series of structural modifications that would allow, once the Tranche 3B was approved, to incorporate the BAE Striker helmet, the AESA CAPTOR radar, the conformable tanks and what concerns us in this entry: the improved EJ200 (in terms of thrust) equipped with 3D vector nozzles (3DTVC, called TV

A real AIM-2000 IRIS-T in a Eurofighter in QRA. [S. Mafé]

The Spanish ITP, company responsible for the convergent-divergent nozzle, is also responsible for the development of the vector nozzle, based on a cardan joint of three concentric rings and joined by four pins. In this nozzle, named as we have already said TVN or Thrust Vectoring Nozzle, each of the concentric rings serves a purpose: the interior is connected to the throat of the nozzle through the second ring forming a cross-shaped connection with the third ring, the pivot, which is connected to the divergent section by means of actuators. The interactions between the different elements of which the nozzle consists allows even improvements in the amount of thrust that it is capable of providing, by acting on the petals of the convergent-divergent nozzle and positioning it and varying its section in various ways. It is therefore necessary that the engine control module, the DECMU, is perfectly integrated with the control software of the Eurofighter, mainly with the element with which it will most interact: the flight control system or FCS (Flight Control System).

The Fuel System

To supply the engines with the vital flow they need, the Eurofighter has an internal fuel capacity estimated at just over 4,500 liters. This is transported in two integral tanks in the fuselage and in the wings in which all the internal space not occupied by structural elements and mechanisms is dedicated to fuel. The wings are "wet" that is, the "skin", in addition to its aerodynamic and structural functions, acts as a tank wall. Given the generous surface area of the wings, one would have to estimate the vulnerability that this represents when faced with small-caliber anti-aircraft fire drilling.

The volume transported internally, is complemented by the use of external tanks that can be placed under the wings and in the central support of the fuselage, which are adapted for the transfer of fuel, ie they are "wet" as well. The "humidity" of those three stations is optional.

In the central support only the tank of 1.000 liters can be installed, while those of the wings admit the 1,000 and the 1,500 liters. These possibilities imply that with the most favorable combination, an additional 4,000 liters can be added to the internal capacity. Although the 1,500-liter tanks come from the Tornado, the 1,000-liter tanks are supersonic and have been specifically designed for the Eurofighter Typhoon by a consortium of which Airbus DS Spain is part. Deposits can be launched in flight within a wide range of envelope values. The TEU (Tank Ejection Unit) launch mechanism is housed in the tank suspension pylon, which is an integral part of the tank, and is controlled by the aircraft's weapon system.

The transfer of fuel between the wings and the tanks of the fuselage is done by means of electromechanical pumps, and by means of air bleed from the engines for the auxiliary tanks. All the fuel transfer is managed by computers that continuously control the fuel content, so that the transfer during transfer between tanks or in the in-flight refueling is done automatically.

Under normal conditions, each engine receives the fuel by means of a feeding booster pump, but in case of failure of one of them, the possibility of cross-feeding is available, that is, the two engines receive fuel by means of a pump, through the front tank of the fuselage.

The fuel, before injecting it into the combustion chamber, is used as a coolant for some mechanical elements such as the hydraulic power "switchboard", the electric generation system and the gearboxes. The heat absorbed by the fuel preheats it, preparing it for combustion, which makes it more efficient.

The refueling, under normal conditions, is carried out under pressure, but it can also be carried out by gravity, should the operational circumstances so require.

As a complement, the Eurofighter Typhoon has for its two variants, the single and the two-seater, a refueling probe in flight that is housed in the right front side of the fuselage next to the windshield. The extension and retraction of the probe is performed hydraulically.

With these combinations, the plane has the following possibilities:

-In the air-ground missions, the radius of action is 650 km. (350 mn.) Transporting seven pumps with a low profile.

-The radius of action almost doubles to more than 1,390 km. (750 mn.) With a Hi-Lo-Lo-Hi profile and three laser guided pumps of 454 kg. (1,000 pounds).

-With the supercruity resource the penetrations in supersonic regime are possible since the use of afterburning is not necessary. The air-air capacity is maintained if it is armed with IRIS-T or AMRAAM even if it carries the external tanks (of 1,000 liters).

-The maximum range of action with a Hi-Lo-Lo-Hi profile is 1,850 km. (1,000 mn) The reach on the transfer (ferry) flights is 3,700 km. (2,000 nm) with the help of three external tanks; one of 1,000 liters, plus two of 1,500 liters.

In comparative terms we will say that the Eurofighter Typhoon has a longer permanence than the F-15. Obviously all these capabilities are enhanced using the in-flight refueling by means of the probe.

The last and interesting novelty regarding the fuel system has been the announcement of the future availability of conformable tanks that can be installed on the sides of the fuselage. This news was announced during the Farnborough Air Show in July 2002, including the display of a full-scale model in which the tanks were installed.

This is an initiative undertaken by BAES jointly with the Australian company GKN Engage. In 2004 the aerodynamic tunnel tests were carried out with a model equipped with the conformable tanks

The combined capacity of both tanks is 1,500 liters and operationally they can be dismantled in 75 minutes. With this additional capacity, the radius of action of the aircraft can be extended by 25%, presenting the additional advantage of freeing the pylons from the wings to install weapons. It is possible to speculate if they will be throwable in flight and how they limit the performance of the airplane, although it has been declared that this reduction is minimal.

Currently, there is no request from any of the current customers for these tanks, but the pre-installation to install them, such as the reinforcements of the fuselage, the wiring and the pipes, were installed from the Tranche 2 aircraft, starting with the production copy number 149, so that the future adoption of these deposits is facilitated for those who want it. Undoubtedly it is possible that it is adopted by some of the air forces of the consortium, and is considered to present an additional attraction for potential customers, especially for air-ground missions where fuel consumption is much higher than in air missions. -Air defense.

Equipment for the mission

The Eurofighter Typhoon has five anchoring points in the fuselage and another four in each wing and can transport up to 6,500 kg. (14,300 pounds) of external charges in its thirteen stations. The basic armament air-air consists of four AMRAAM missiles that are installed in semi-

The Spanish ITP, company responsible for the convergent-divergent nozzle, is also responsible for the development of the vector nozzle, based on a cardan joint of three concentric rings and joined by four pins. [Eurojet]

Specifications	
Dimensions:	
Total length:	15.96 m.
Total height:	5.28 m.
Wingspan:	10.95 m
Lengthening the Wing:	2,2
Surface alar:	50 m2
Surface flat front:	2.4 m2
Alar Load:	306 Kg./m2
Pesos:	
Thrust / weight ratio:	1.2
Empty weight:	10,995 Kg.
Maximum takeoff weight:	21,000 kg.
Internal fuel load:	4,500 kg.
External loads (weapons and fuel):	6,500 - 8,000 kg.
Benefits	
Maximum speed:	2,125 km / h (Mach 2.0)
Time at 10,670 m:	2.5 minutes
Landing run:	700 m
Take-off mission combat mission:	300 m.
Combat radio attack on the ground lo-lo-lo:	601 km.
Battle radius ground attack lo-lo-hi:	1,389 km.
Air defense with 3 h. CAP:	185 km.
Air defense with 10 minute loitering:	1389 km.
Limits of G, with internal fuel and two AIM-120:	+ 9 / -3
Maximum published ceiling:	18,044 m.
Engine specifications	
ISA conditions, not installed, by motor.	
Maximum thrust with afterburning:	90 kN (20,000 pounds)
Maximum thrust without afterburning:	60 kN (13,500 pounds)
Combustion system:	Injected by vaporization.
Average specific consumption with maximum thrust without afterburning:	21-23 g / kNS
With afterburning:	47-49 g / kNS
Total length:	4.00 m.
Diameter of the admission:	0,74 m.
Basic weight with afterburner:	990-1035 Kg. (2,180-2,286 lbs)
Stages of the compressor:	3 low pressure, 5 high pressure.
Stages of the turbine:	1 low pressure, 1 high pressure.
Sustainability Criteria	
Reliability	
Attributable defects per 1,000 flight hours	<400
Probability of completing the mission successfully	> 95%
Probability of autonomous start-up of engine	> 98%
Maintainability	
Hours / maintenance man per flight hour	<9
Defects rectified in 45 minutes:	50%
Engine change for four people:	45 minutes
Defects rectified in three hours:	90%
Service	
Pre-flight inspection:	<15 minutes / two people
Walkaround:	<15 minutes / two people
Post-flight inspection:	<45 minutes / two people
Monitoring of Defects	
False alarm rate:	<5%
100% of critical failures for safety will be detected	
Changes of Mission	
<45 minutes / three people any change.	
Air-air configuration:	<23 minutes / six people
Air-ground configuration:	<30 minutes (six people)
Scheduled maintenance	
Minimum interval 400 flight hours or 24 months, whichever happens first.	
Ability to grow	
Growth is an inherent part of the Eurofighter Typhoon. Since the beginning of the program, the appearance of obsolescence was considered a major factor for a 21st century aircraft. All the main components of the airplane have a large capacity incorporated for the inclusion of future enhancements in a profitable manner.	
This philosophy is intimately linked with the capacity of the improvement program that has been designed for the future, to ensure that the aircraft retains the ability to overcome its potential adversaries throughout its life cycle.	
When in 2005 the Eurofighter Typhoon reached full operational capacity (FOC), the following growth capacity was still available:	
Volume for Electronic equipment:	10%
Engine thrust:	15%
Electric power:	25%
Environmental control system: 25%	
Data bus load: 100%	
Computer memory: 100%	
Avionics growth: 100%	

Air-Air Armament: 100%

NOTE: The values given below must be taken with due precautions. Many of them are estimates or data made public long ago so they may have been revised, due to the airplane's natural progress. "As a rule," it should be assumed that a military aircraft always has better performance than those published.

embedded supports in the lower corners of the fuselage to reduce resistance. The origin of this type of installation can be traced to the F-4 and has had its continuity in the tornado. In addition, the aircraft can use two short-range missiles such as the AIM-9L, ASRAAM or IRIS-T on the external wing supports. This initial combination has been replaced in the by the Meteor/ ASRAAM and the IRIS-T, depending on the nation that requests it.

The use of air-to-air weapons of North American origin has been controversial because of the limitations in the transfer of technology that the Americans could impose, especially in the face of exports. This aspect seems to be solved and except in exceptional cases, the Eurofighter can use the AIM-120 without more limitations than the logics for exports.

The State Department, as the executive agency for the issuance of all licenses for the use of military equipment, had no objections in principle to the export proposals of the BVRAAM based on the AMRAAM.

The US Government supports the transfer of the BVRAAMs based on AMRAAM to all members of the Eurofighter consortium and Sweden.

The US Government will consider the transfer of the BVRAAMs based on the AMRAAMs to the countries authorized for the AMRAAM.

The US Air Force will sponsor the activity required for the issuance of authorizations. Applications for export to countries not authorized for AMRAAM will be considered on a case-by-case basis.

The US Air Force did not take any action against the granting of authorizations prior to the selection of the BVRAAM (Meteor) based on the AMRAAM.

This document prompted the following statements from Andy Head, Director of Marketing of Raytheon: «This is an unprecedented movement that shows that the US is determined, once and for all, to eliminate any obstacle and remains of doubts that no the technology on which the AMRAAMs are based will be retained, in the commercial competitions between the US and Europe. In addition, the United States will cooperate with the Ministry of Defense of the United Kingdom in the development of exports from the United Kingdom of the BVRAAM based on the AMRAAM. This is good news for future sales of the Eurofighter and will safeguard and create thousands of jobs in Europe. "

"Given that AMRAAM is already in service in 16 nations, and approved for 22, including the Associated Nations, Saudi Arabia and most of the NATO countries, it is conceivable that there will be some country to which the Eurofighter consortium nations will not be able to export the aircraft equipped with the BVRAAM. However, the cases of Greece and Norway are a good test in which the AMRAAM ensures that the Eurofighter has the capacity that customers require to compete with other fighters. Only the Raytheon

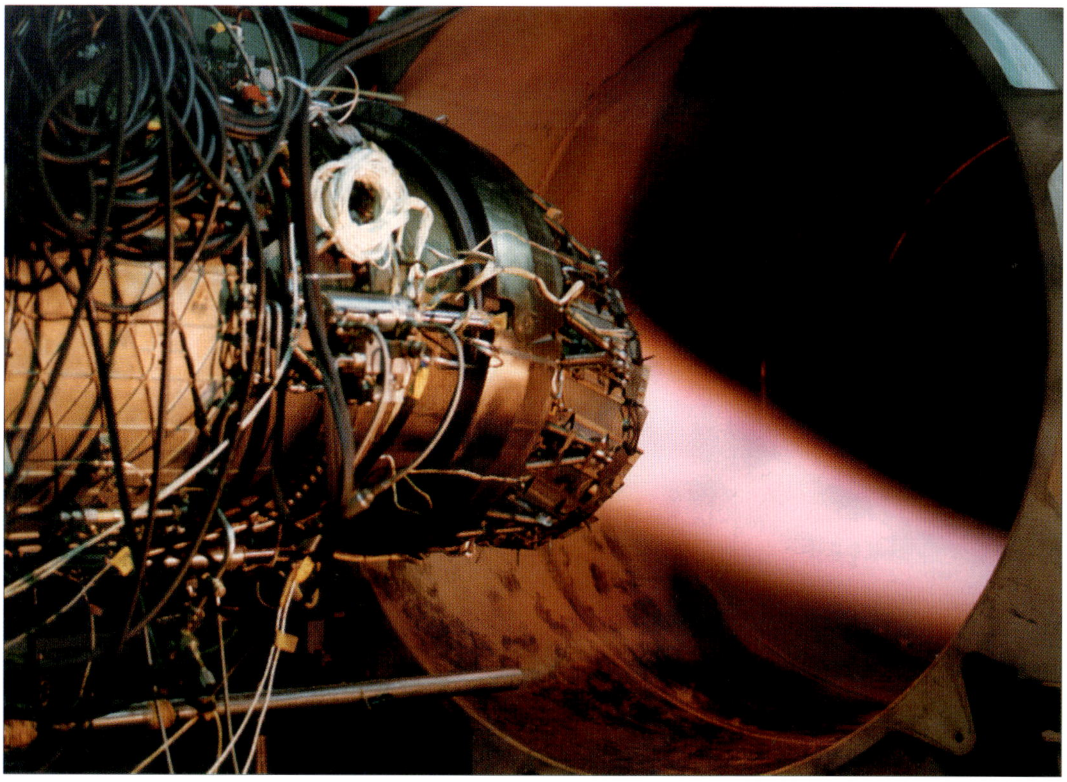

In this nozzle, named as we have already said TVN or Thrust Vectoring Nozzle, each of the concentric rings serves a purpose: the interior is connected to the throat of the nozzle through the second ring forming a shaped connection of cross joint with the third ring, the pivot, which is connected to the divergent section by means of actuators. [Eurojet]

BVRAAM provides the Eurofighter with a crucial competitive advantage for export, until the arrival of the Meteor that increases them. "

These statements should serve as "removes fears" to future interested in the acquisition of Eurofighter.

In 2004-2009 about 1,000 ARA-120B AMRAAM missiles were acquired by Germany, Spain, England and Italy, to equip the Eurofighter, on the other hand and as a complement to the Meteor the consortium is receiving (2018-2020) the most advanced AIM- 120C5 / 7 for air superiority missions. Evidently Raytheon has been supporting the Eurofighter consortium in the integration program.

The economic impact of the eurofighter program in Spain

20,000 jobs created and sustained in Spain (all phases of development, production, support, and counting direct aerospace sectors, related to the supply chain and indirect / other industrial or economic).

+ 40% of the Gross Contract Value (VAT from the contract, other taxes, contribution to social security) returned to public funds of the State.

From its beginnings, the Spanish participation in the so-called EFA project (European Fighter Aircraft) has been a central element in the development of defense technologies. In the years 1992, 93, 94, 95, 96 and 97 the percentage of the defense ID destined to the EFA was 73%, 68% 54%, 44%, 44% and 84% respectively, with an approximate amount of 200,000 million pesetas (1,202 million Euros). And also, we already know the important role that Spanish R & D of defense represents within the public budgets of R & D, which is around 20%.

At the sectoral level, Eurofighter was expected to activate three areas: the creation of new companies, the increase of technological capabilities and the provision of test centers and technical assistance. To carry out the project, the government created in 1989 two companies, the Turbo Propulsion Industry (ITP), for the manufacture of engines; the Spanish Company of Aeronautical Systems (CESA), for the manufacture of pneumatic and fuel equipment.

The important thing is to know if Eurofighter has achieved technological and industrial benefits for Spain. In any case, the truth is that until now there has been a large investment of public funds, justified by the appeal to defend the country and its model of society; Finally, it can be said that the program has been a success, despite delays and costs. So far we know that many of the subcontractor companies of Airbus Defense & Space and ITP are subsidiaries of foreign companies whose installation in Spain was "ad hoc" for the Eurofighter project.

One of the main implications of the project are the economic consequences. If we compare the Spanish defense budgets with respect to the other partner countries, Spanish military spending would be -in terms of GDP- lower than those of Germany, Italy and Great Britain. The budget of the EFA on total public investment in defense has reached over 40 years of 40% of total state

The interactions between the different elements of which the nozzle consists allows even improvements in the amount of thrust that is able to provide, by acting on the petals of the convergent-divergent nozzle and position and vary its section in various ways. [Eurojet]

The first single-seater prototype to fly was the DA1, built by MBB at its factory in Manching. It made his first flight on March 27, 1994 with test pilot Peter Weger at the controls. [Eurofighter]

investments. And until 1995, only 16.8% of the total planned for the project had been invested. The Spanish government undertook to acquire a total of 87 aircraft -71 single-seaters and 16 two-seaters-, which was subsequently reduced to 73, to finally include an additional 40 (still without budgeting).

The Ministry of Defense estimates that around 30% of the final cost will return to the state coffers through the corresponding part of taxes and social security of the companies involved, and expects benefits with future exports.

The sectors that assume most of the contracting (99% in total) are aerospace and electronic and IT.

The three defining features

There are three facets that define the Spanish participation in the Eurofighter project:

1st) The political consensus, argued by the considered necessary renovation of the Air Force.

2nd) The new sensitivity of the threat to security in the Mediterranean area.

3rd) And the willingness to belong to European or international initiatives in the interstate defense organizations or in the United Nations.

In any case, it must be said first:

a) The modernization of weapons systems has its budgetary limits, which in the case of the Eurofighter seem to have been widely overcome.

b) The problems of the Mediterranean area are more economic, social and cultural than not military, and in consequence political actions should focus more towards cooperation or mutual aid and understanding, which did not extend the defense. However, all this changed at the end of the last decade, and especially with the appearance of non-state actors, such as the various jihadist organizations, in addition to the aggressive policy of Russia.

c) Participation in international programs of research, development and production of new weapons systems has not been the subject of public debate in Spain due to the lack of tradition of military problems in a country that until very recently was considered only for "experts", not extendable to public opinion. It has been believed and created, with unquestioned faith, in all kinds of internationalisms, and that participation in this program reaffirmed an industrial policy option.

Second, we must underline:

Technological innovation, as one of the most important eleme a) Technological innovation, as one of the elements that has had more weight against public opinion on the part of the administration, as of the entrepreneurs. For this, three arguméntales lines were established: 1ª) the economies of scale derived from the joint works of R & D; 2nd) technology transfers and acquisition of new skills of Spanish companies; 3rd) the creation of research infrastructures by providing greater capacities to existing or new centers.

And in third and last place:

In its beginnings, Eurofighter represented 8.7% of the activity of the defense industry and 12.4% of the aerospace industry, which represented 2.2% and 1.6% respectively of the industrial production of the country and have resulted in 1.3% and 0.6% of jobs in the secondary sector. With the serial production of the 73 aircraft, more components for the rest of the international fleet, industrial activity tripled. A project like this, has allowed a more than acceptable number of Spanish companies to participate in it, which led to its modernization to the latest standards are: Airbus Defense & Space and ITP with significant participation in the program: ENOSA, CESA, TECNOBIT, PAGE IBERICA, DRAEGER HISPANIA, INTA, FIBERTECNIC, NAC COMPANY. SANTA BARBARA, GAMESA, CONSUR, BERU MICROELECTRÓNICA, J.V.C. SPAIN, SAINSEL, MICROTECNICA and EINSA Another 288 national or international companies act as subcontractors of the previous 19.

During the summer of 2000, the DA2, changed its elegant scheme of air superiority, based on two shades of gray, with a striking, and intriguing, all-enveloping black scheme. This change of livery led more than one observer to think enthusiastically. Ah, finally the Stealth Eurofighter! However, the reason for the change in color was much more related to cosmetics and aesthetics, than to an enigmatic and furtive variant, as we will see below. Indeed, during the summer-fall of 2000, the DA2 was used within the Flight Load Assessment program. This series of tests, aimed at the preparation of the pressure tables generated on the carbon fiber structures of the cell, during maneuvers with high G numbers and low speed. [Eurofighter]

Development

The Eurofighter Typhoon is a versatile, twin-engine, highly maneuverable fighter designed and built by the Eurofighter GmbH consortium of European companies, created in 1983 and composed of the companies Airbus Military, BAE Systems and Leonardo. He made his first flight on March 27, 1994, entering service on April 8, 2003 in Germany. Its design with delta-canard wing configuration resembles that of other modern combat aircraft such as Dassault Rafale, from France, and Saab 39 Gripen, from Sweden. It was designed thinking that its combination of agility, furtive capabilities and advanced aviation systems would categorize it as one of the best fighters currently in service.

The serial production of the Eurofighter Typhoon has been divided into three phases (or tranches), with a gradual increase of the aircraft's capabilities in each of them. It is in service with the British RAF, the German Luftwaffe, the Italian Aeronautica Militare, the Spanish Air Force and the Austrian Air Force, the Royal Air Force of Saudi Arabia and the Sultanate of Oman, as well as Kuwait and Qatar have also studied orders

The DA2 before being painted black. [Eurofighter]

The project was initiated by a technical requirement from several countries to replace SEPECAT Jaguar, Panavia Tornado, McDonnell Douglas

F-4 Phantom II, Lockheed F-104 Starfighter and Dassault Mirage F1 of various European air forces. The trigger for the appearance of this new fighter was, among others, the information that was being received about the new Soviet prototypes RAM-K and RAM-L, which would later be known as Su-27 Flanker and MiG-29 Fulcrum. The aircraft was designed taking into account the technical requirements of the air forces of some NATO members such as Germany, France and the United Kingdom. However, the French air force soon abandoned the project when they wanted to build a custom-made aircraft where Dassault led the design and the other partners limited themselves to jointly financing the project. Furthermore, the Armée del Air was not satisfied with designs such as the TFK -90 or the P110B, on which the Eurofighter is based, preferring a somewhat smaller and embarcable aircraft, which is why France abandoned the European aircraft project, to create its own fighter, the ACX (acronym for Combat Expérimental Aircraft) , that later would happen to be known as Rafale.

DA6 and DA7 flying over Paris; It was the first time that two Eurofighters were flying in formation. [Eurofighter]

In this way, in 1982 the ACA (Agile Combat Aircraft) program was presented, in which Germany, Italy and the United Kingdom appeared as partners. We tried to create a program for a technological demonstrator called EAP (Experimental Aircraft Program), but the British government did not finance it and in the end it had to be the BAe (British Aerospace) itself that financed the project, taking advantage of parts such as the tail section of the Tornado and its RB199 engines. The EAP made its first flight in 1986 and was immediately successful. There were some voices that wanted that same plane to enter service in the Royal Air Force (RAF), but the development of the more conservative Tornado F3 stopped the financing of the project. However, Germany also developed then the X-31 along with the American company Rockwell to have technologies applicable to the future ACA, although the newest, the 3D adjustable nozzle of the same did not equip the Eurofigther, at least at first . The Eurofighter departs to a large extent from technologies tested in the EAP.

Spain joined the project on September 2, 1985, although it had followed with interest the evolution of events. From then on the project was known as EFA (European Fighter Aircraft) and several consortiums were formed to carry out

Perspective of the DA6, an example of development built in Spain, and which was the only prototype to suffer an accident. [Eurofighter]

the various parts of the Eurofighter aircraft: for cell and system integration, for Eurojet engines, for the EuroDASS security system, etc. . From then on, the project suffered a break due to the end of the Cold War and the high costs of German reunification, which meant that the project was delayed for about five years. Meanwhile, the partners discussed ways to reduce the price of the plane, as well as the overall cost of the program, by eliminating systems from the aircraft (for example: the very high protection against pulses of electromagnetic radiation), or by reducing the number of prototypes. Finally, on March 27, 1994, the first DA01 prototype flew from the MBB factory in Manching with test driver Peter Weger at the controls. For eight years the seven prototypes of the program made numerous flight hours to reach the manufacturing phase at the beginning of 2001.

When the final production contract was signed, the revised sales were: United Kingdom 232 apparatuses, Germany 180, Italy 121 and Spain 87 (for a total amount of 10.795 million euros). The production was redistributed according to the following percentages: British Aerospace (37%), DASA (29%), Aeritalia (19.5%) and CASA (he development is the responsibility of Eurofighter Jagdflugzeug GmbH, based in Munich, a company wholly owned by BAE Systems (part of British Aerospace) in the United Kingdom, Leonardo in Italy, EADS Deutschland Aerospace Group (owned by Daimler Chrysler in conjunction with DASA) and Airbus Military (formerly CASA). Currently, Germany and Spain are part of the Airbus Military consortium.

The project has been named and renamed several times since its birth, being known as EFA (European Fighter Aircarft), Eurofighter, EF2000 (Eurofighter 2000) and Typhoon

The acronyms DA and IPA designate the two types of platforms used in the Eurofighter program for flight tests.

This program includes a total of 4,700 flight hours dedicated to tests to be carried out by the DAs and IPAs, although it is a value that is subject to continuous review, depending on the needs.

The DAs can be considered the prototypes of the program and seven copies have been built that have been numbered DA1 to DA7 consecutively. Initially eight prototypes were programmed, but in 1991 and as a measure to reduce costs, one of them was canceled, a two-seater that would have been the third English test aircraft. This fact was the reason why the designations initially reserved for each airplane suffered some "displacements" to accommodate this reduction. These airplanes, which began to fly with basic configurations, some of them still with Tornado engines, adapted and limited in performance, were updated progressively as different systems and equipment became available. His story is that of the Eurofighter development program.

Development Aircraft

DA1: The first single-seater prototype to fly was the DA1, built by MBB at its Manching factory. He made his first flight on March 27, 1994 with test driver Peter Weger at the controls. Afterwards, the fuselage codes 98 + 29 were applied. Initially it was thought that this prototype would be based on Warton, so it reserved the English military serial number ZH586, this finally never happened, although the aircraft did deploy incidentally to this base in 1997 to perform test flights in supersonic regime.

The DA1 flew with the first version of the software for the FCS.

This prototype had planned to conduct 635 experimental flights and has been used, mainly

The DA4 showing the generous braking parachute, which by the way, is rarely used. [Eurofighter]

This is the only prototype built by Spain and the second of the two-seaters. Its designation must have been DA7. Its first flight was made on August 31, 1996 in Getafe, piloted by Alfonso de Miguel, the Flight Operations Director of the then EADS CASA. This aircraft was ahead of the British two-seater, although it is true that this flight was made with some delay compared to the initial forecasts, due to the checks to which the software of the FCS Phase 2A was submitted. It had to carry out 315 flights dedicated to checking the flight handling characteristics and the environmental control system. It received registration XCE.16-01.
In March 2002 was was dedicated to testing the handling qualities in the subsonic regime and the Auto Low Speed Recovery subsystem (ALSR), plus tests of the DVI (Direct Voice Input), and Avionics and Systems for the two-seater. In October 2002, DA6 was at the Morón air base (after the DA1), to perform various flight tests; a month later it crashed in the province of Toledo, because the SW and DECU (Digital Engine Control Unit) caused a bad activation of the dynamic outlets of the engines, causing them to shut down. The pilots (Cuadrado and Lombo) were able to eject. It was temporarily replaced in Getafe by the DA1. [S. Mafé]

The DA2 was subjected to a series of rigorous tests, receiving special instrumentation, which consisted of a digital tape recorder, which was located in the nose radome and a modified digital video recorder. The first records the uniform pressures and the second the irregular pressures, instead of video images.

by DASA, for flight and engine handling tests. At the end of 1998 the DA1 had made 123 flights and was in the Manching workshops in an out-of-service condition to install the EJ200 engines, replacing the RB199 with which it had begun to fly. With this same model of engine had reached Mach 1.94 during the handling tests in supersonic regime. The aircraft had already carried out braking tests with high and low speed hooks.

During this stoppage, it was also used to install the Martin Baker Mk16 ejection seat and the standard avionics package 3910. In 2001, it carried out the refueling in the buddy-buddy mode with a Tornado.

In April 2002, the DA1 had accumulated 271.8 hours over 332 flights. This prototype has been penalized by two long periods of immobilization due to the introduction of successive improvements. The first one related to the update of the flight control system software, followed by another derivative of the installation of the EJ200 engines and the update of its avionics.

DA2: Less than a month apart, he made the first flight on April 6, 1994 from the tracks of Warton, the second single-seat prototype built by BAE. This first flight was delayed due to the bad weather and the double checks to which it was subjected to the software, especially necessary in view of the losses of one of the prototypes of the Gripen, of a YF-22 plus an MV-22. All of them lost associated with software failures not previously detected. It received registration number ZH588. His assigned assignment in the program is that of the expansion of the flight envelope and has been one of the most active aircraft of all the prototypes. The DA2 is assigned the realization of 575 flights.

During the show of Paris of 1995, the DA2 made an appearance in the static parking of airplanes decorated with a large numeral 270, remaining in exhibition only a few days. Alleging many compromises with the flight test program, he disappeared one afternoon to Warton. This was the first public appearance of the Eurofighter.

As a rematch perhaps, the DA2 was given the honor of making the first public appearance (in flight) of the Eurofighter, during the Farnborough show in September 1996. With BAE's pilot test pilot, John Turner. Despite being equipped with the RB199 Mk104E engines, which provide 20% less thrust than the final EJ200, the flight routine was impressive. High-speed turns (6G) were included at a speed of 591 km / h and a no less impressive take-off; The plane was in the air five seconds after the release of brakes with a speed of 203 km / h!

During the summer of 2000, the DA2, changed its elegant scheme of air superiority, based on two shades of gray, a striking, and intriguing, all-enveloping black scheme. This change of livery led more than one observer to think enthusiastically. Ah, finally the Eurofighter Stealth! However, the reason for the change in color was much more related to cosmetics and aesthetics, than to an enigmatic and furtive variant, as we will see below.

Indeed, during the summer-fall of 2000, the DA2 was used within the Flight Load Assessment program. This series of tests, aimed at the preparation of the pressure tables generated on the carbon fiber structures of the cell, during maneuvers with high G numbers and low speed.

In this way, the loads to which they are subjected were evaluated, certain areas of the aircraft. For this purpose, 490 pressure transducers were installed, distributed in the fuselage, to measure the stress values at the points chosen by the engineers. Most of them were installed on the right side of the plane.

Each of the transducers, (which are the size of a small button), is installed on the skin of the plane surrounded by a rubber disc, and is connected to the recording instrumentation, through multiplexers, by means of a cable flat. Each transducer, its disc and corresponding cable, were embedded in the skin of the plane to avoid the generation of undesirable aerodynamic disturbances.

Typhoon

Typhoon

Typhoon

In spite of that, the aspect of the airplane plagued of 490 whitish patches and its corresponding wiring was not too elegant. Therefore and to disguise the little aesthetic effect, the paint scheme was changed to black. This provides greater visibility, and achieves an additional aerodynamic seal for the transducers. Otherwise the plane would have appeared to be under the influence of a strong attack of smallpox.

These test flights were made from the base of RAF Leuchars in August. The initial tests were carried out in the basic configuration consisting of four AIM-120 AMRAAM missiles and two AIM-9L Sidewinders. Followed by another series of tests with fuel tanks installed under the wings.

The instrumentation that was installed to the DA2 for these tests consisted of a digital tape recorder, which was located in the nose radome and a modified digital video recorder. The first records the uniform pressures and the second the irregular pressures, instead of video images. The uniform pressures are those that change with the speed of the plane, altitude and angle of attack, while the irregular pressures are those generated by the local turbulences and fluctuate more quickly, they are generated due to the turbulences that occur in the boundary layer stuck to the skin of the plane. Its effects are more significant with large angles of attack or with the deployed airbrake and can generate vibrations (buffeting) due to the irregular flow of air. Depending on their level, they are detectable locally or if they are very strong, they can be felt by the pilot. In both cases it is an undesirable circumstance. The first flight within the Cargo Supervision program was held on July 28, 2000. By mid-October, the DA2 had made 39 flights to benefit this program, followed by another eight in mid-November.

In December 2000, the plane carried out the refueling (dry) of fuel in flight from a Tornado and a Tristar. Later it was put out of service to make some updates, among which as most notable is the installation of the EJ200-03Z engines and production standards, which replaced the -03Y and final development variants. This aircraft, which has consistently remained the most active in the fleet, had accumulated more than 300 flights during the year 2001, and has sometimes flown four times on the same day. Among the achievements of this prototype are the flight to Mach 2, on December 23, 1997 and the achievement of a roof of 15,240 m. (50,000 feet) in April 1999, equipped with the Aircrew Services Package (ASP), which was the expected standard for use in production aircraft, representing the fact an important stage in the expansion of the aircraft's capabilities at high altitude. The ASP has the mission of providing breathing under pressure at altitude, which protects the pilot from conditions at high altitude (low environmental pressure) and during maneuvers with accelerations (G). In June of 2001, and with the new motorization, it was reincorporated to the test plan, continuing with the expansion of the flight envelope. The most recent achievement of the DA2 has been the conclusion of the tests, announced on July 23, 2002, corresponding to the Carefree Handling program. These tests are designed to evaluate the behavior of the aircraft's FCS.

"Careless Driving" means that the pilot can perform any action he wishes with the lever, pedals and engine acceleration control, confident that the Flight Control System (FCS) will protect the aircraft, and consequently the crew member,

The Eurofighter Typhoon is a multipurpose, twin-engine and highly manoeuvrable fighter, designed and built by the consortium of European companies Eurofighter GmbH, created in 1983 and composed of companies Airbus Defence & Space, BAE Systems and Leonardo. It made his first flight on March 27, 1994, entering service on April 8, 2003 in Germany. Its design with delta-canard wing configuration resembles that of other modern combat aircraft such as Dassault Rafale, from France, and Saab 39 Gripen, from Sweden. It was designed thinking that its combination of agility, furtive capabilities and advanced aviation systems will categorize it as one of the best fighters currently in service, with an outstanding purity of lines. [Eurofighter]

One of the IPA with colors of the Luftwaffe and dedicated to the test of armament, loaded with AIM-120 AMRAAM, AIM-2000 IRIS-T and bombs guided by laser. [Eurofighter]

maintaining the flight parameters such as angle of attack, acceleration forces (G) and bank rate, within safe levels.

To test the FCS completely, the aircraft is installed the most demanding configuration of weapons, which are asymmetric. In this specific case, two Advanced Medium Range air-to-air missiles and a short-range Sidewinder missile were installed under the DA2 fuselage stations on the right-hand rail. Later in the process to get full operational capacity, other combinations were tested. The DA2 is the only one of the seven prototypes that could perform these tests.

This is possible because during the third phase of test flights, from the end of 1997 to the beginning of 1998, the recovery mechanism of augers was installed by means of a braking parachute. These tests are now concluded. The first flight control system of the Eurofighter was called Phase 0 and corresponded with the FCS which was to serve as the last emergency system and which in fact amounted to a very basic flight control. This circumstance served so that in their day the usual malicious observers raised the comment that the Eurofighter "had made its initial flights using the emergency system".

For the full authorization of the FCS, six progressive phases of improvements to the initial software were planned.

The pilot responsible for concluding this phase was Craig Penrice. He stated "Flying careless driving tests is the most exciting of the flight tests because you are taking the plane and your software to its limits."

"The flight control system has behaved entirely as predicted during aerodynamic tunnel testing and simulation. This wonderful achievement is a credit to everyone involved. "

DA3: Just one year after the second prototype did it, in June 1995, the Italian plane with

The Spanish IPA4, C.16-20 / 11-91, during the extreme cold tests in northern Sweden. [Eurofighter]

the MMX602 license plate, built by Aeritalia in Turin-Caselle, was flying. The pilot responsible for putting the DA3 on the air was commander Napoleone Bragagnolo, at the time Director of Flight Operations at Alenia.

This prototype, also single-seater, was destined according to the initial plans to be the DA4 and made 490 flights of test. Its main mission was to carry out the tests of engines, armament (cannon firing) and launching of under-loads. He was the first to fly with the EJ200 engine. The first 40 flights were made with two EJ200-01A engines, which we could define as the initial development standard and which would be later replaced by the -01C version, capable of providing 5% more thrust, which translates into that already met 95% of the expected benefits. In May of 1997, the EJ200-3A initial production standards were installed. The DA3, depending on the assignments assigned, was the first Eurofighter to fly with fuel tanks installed under the wings.

he Eurofighter can transport a maximum of three suspended fuel tanks. The possible combinations are a deposit of 1,000 liters in the central support of the fuselage and other two, which can be 1,000 or 1,500 liters, under the wings. With large tanks installed, the aircraft is restricted to subsonic flight.

The first public appearance of the DA3 and also the first demonstration of the Eurofighter in Italy, was held in Practica di Mare, on the occasion of the celebration of the 75th Anniversary of the Italian Military Aviation, which happened in May 1998. The first tests of detachment of the additional tanks in flight would take place on June 17 of the same year 1998.

Anecdotally we will say that during the initial tests of the engines the Eurofighter entered the supercruise regime (supersonic flight without afterburning) accidentally. The plane was flying at 12,200 meters and at a speed of 1.4 Mach, with 50% of its fuel capacity and loaded with six simulated missiles. The afterburner was cut after the required acceleration until the supersonic regime, when, to the surprise of the pilot, the aircraft continued flying to Mach 1+.

In 1999 he finished the tests of initial certification of the engines, previously had been installed in Caselle during the month of October the engines of the production version -03Z. Among the achievements of that year it can be mentioned that in December he flew in a supersonic regime (Mach 1.6) with 3 tanks of 1,000 liters installed under the wings, corroborating the increase in services offered by the new engines. Previously this same plane had managed to exceed Mach 1 with the three tanks in February, and in March it reached Mach 1.6 with two 1,000-liter tanks under the wings. It should be added that these tests were performed with functional deposits and not mere aerodynamic bulges under the wings.

The DA2 and the DA3 were the first two aircraft to which the first improvement of the Flight Control System software was retro-fitted, which allowed for the replenishment of air-to-air fuel and the installation of fuel tanks under the wings. This is equivalent to the revised mode of the final version of the software.

On March 20, 2002, the DA3 conducted the firing tests of the Mauser Bk 27 cannon of the aircraft and the vibrations generated in the pro-

The IPA4 was built by the then EADS-CASA. Analysis of performances and flight qualities in Air-Air and Air-Surface configurations, including "carefree-handling" and "flutter" in the latter, Air-Surface weapon integration (GBU 10/16), environmental tests and MIDS verification , is PS001 C.16.20 / 11-91, it was retrofitted to Tranche 2 and later to 3A. There is also an ISPA (Instrumented Production Aircraft), which is the ST010 CE.16-10 / 11-79, lent to Airbus, based on Getafe.

cess. A blast of 30 projectiles was fired (from the ground) with satisfactory results.

DA4: The first two-seater built, but not the first to fly was the DA4, also manufactured by BAE in Warton. His first flight dates back to March 14, 1997 and he received registration number ZH590. This aircraft in turn was designated to be the DA3. Within the program, it was planned to carry out more than 420 flights dedicated to the development and integration of the ECR 90 radar and to the flight handling tests of the two-seater version.

One of the first tests to which the DA4 was submitted, as soon as it was delivered, would be those of compatibility with the reinforced refuges for airplanes. These took place from July 18 to 25, 1997, developing at the base of the RAF of Leeming and in some way reveal, how modern airplanes with their high technological content, they become precious objects to be taken care of.

In principle, the tests were promoted due to the concern generated about the adequacy of the shelters used by the RAF when the DA2 was diverted to the aforementioned base in 1995, so it was considered necessary to carry out the relevant tests as soon as it could be available. airplane. The purpose of the tests was to evaluate the impact of noise and vibration caused by the engine inside the shelter on both the aircraft and the personnel. In order to carry out the necessary measures, sensors (accelerometers) were installed in the aircraft structure to measure vibration and resonance during engine tests.

A concern associated with this problem was the possible impact on the base environment. The Eurofighter has proven to be noisier and have higher vibration levels than the Tornado F3 that was the usual resident of the base.

The tests revealed advantages and disadvantages. The smaller size of the Eurofighter allows two planes to be placed in a row inside the shelter, instead of tilted as required by the F3 Tornado. The low location of the air intakes for the engines makes it more prone to damage by ingestion of foreign objects (FOD), during the start-ups inside the shelter, which can be easily resolved by keeping the shelter floor clean. Another problem revealed and that particularly displeases the gunsmiths, is the low height of the wing, which makes it difficult to place the ammunition in the supports, especially the AIM-9L / AIM-132 ASRAAM / AIM-2000 IRIS-T.

Additionally, the access doors to the engines can not be opened with the missiles installed in the rear supports of the fuselage, the same as with the Tornado, so any work on the engines involves dismantling the weapons if it is installed.

During the month of April 1999 DA4 undertook a demonstration tour through England, Germany and Italy, in order that a number of high ranking officers, as representatives of the participating air forces, could experience the aircraft in flight. All the guests were able to fly as planned. A total of 16 flights were made, experiencing only two setbacks; a blowout of a wheel and a minor hydraulic failure, which if one thinks that it was a prototype in the development phase, is a good tribute to the progressive maturity of the a In February of 2000, the DA4 was registered his flight number 75 and that agreed with the 1,000 hours of test of the program and it had an active ejectable rear seat. During 2001, the initial evaluation of the GPWS began.

The mention of the operating rear seat gives us the opportunity to mention the completion of the ejection tests of both the rear and front seats with success in January 2002 at the Martin Baker industrial estate at Langford Lodge. The tests were conducted from a front section of a Eurofighter installed on a rail and propelled by a rocket motor at the speed of 600 knots (1111 km / h) at sea level and which is the highest speed at which they were tested.

During March 2002, the DA4 performed the longest test flight recorded to date, with a duration of four hours and 22 minutes, the first "wet" refueling from a VC-10 of the RAF on night flight. The DA4 was equipped with two external tanks. The successful development of these tests was considered as a prerequisite to undertake the first launch of an AMRAAM.

On April 9, 2002, another important test was made for the progress and credibility of the Eurofighter, this consisted in the guided launch against a flying target of an AIM-120 missile, an ingenuity of the BVR class. (Beyond Visual Range). The ECR 90 radar acquired the target at very long distance (30 km) by continuously monitoring until the missile was fired destroying the target. The missile was fired "in the face" with a "look-down" launch geometry against an Italian-built Mirach 100 sub-scale drone powered by a turbojet engine. Although the missile did not have war load on its warhead but telemetry equipment, the target was hit completely and therefore destroyed by the simple kinetic energy of the impact. The tests were conducted on a polygon that the British Ministry of Defense has in the waters near the Hebridean Islands. The pilot at the controls was Craig Penrice.

The importance of the test lies in the fact that the Eurofighter has been designed around the armament of the BVR class, therefore showing its capacity to use it is paramount. This essay comes to complete the previous releases made in the polygon of Salto di Quirra (Decimomannu) by the DA7.

The departure was supported by a BAE Tornado as an observer aircraft, an RAF tanker based on Brize Norton and a maritime search Nimrod, turning the event into a team effort.

The DA4 also performed the DASS system tests in flight operating from the Northumberland electronic warfare site. Previously the aircraft had already completed the first phase of DASS ground tests during the year 2001 in the electronic warfare facilities of Warton.

DA5: It should have been the third prototype built by BAE, but its cancellation allowed this designation to be applied to the second German aircraft and fifth of the prototypes, which in turn had to be designated DA6. The first flight was made on February 24, 1997 from Manching. As the DA4 was dedicated to the development and integration tests of the ECR 90 radar, being the first of the prototypes to fly with the one installed from the beginning. In fact, during the first flight of one hour, the radar, in its standard version C, was fully operational and followed several echoes. It had planned to make 385 flights, although until its withdrawal made some more, and EJ200-3A engines of standard production were installed.

Beginning on May 18, 1999, the DA5 made the 1,000th flight of the program with Wolfgang Schirdewahn as a pilot. At that time the 830 flight hours had been completed and at least 90% of the flight envelope required for the Initial Operational Capacity had been explored. This 1,000 flight was the culmination of an intense period in which 62 flights had been completed in the preceding five weeks.

Also during 1999, the DA5 received, by then the latest version of the software for the FCS, designated FCS 2B/1, which included the functions of auto-throttle, autopilot and With habitual base in Manching, was deployed in March of 2001, to the base of the Luftwaffe of Laage to realize practices of operation of the radar. The Lufwaffe provided up to 20 MiG-29 and F-4F Phantom to simulate complex air-to-air scenarios in which the radar Captor demonstrated excellent performance in acquisition distance and contact tracking accuracy.

DA6: This is the only prototype built by Spain and the second of the two-seater. His designation must have been DA7. Its first flight was made on August 31, 1996 in Getafe, piloted by Alfonso de Miguel, the Flight Operations Director of the then EADS CASA. This aircraft was ahead of the English two-seater, although it is true that this flight was made with some delay compared to the initial forecasts, due to the checks to which the software of the FCS Phase 2A was submitted. It had to carry out 315 flights dedicated to checking the flight handling characteristics and the environmental control system. He received registration XCE.16-01.

During the 1997 aeronautical show in Paris, the DA6 and the DA7 were presented publicly, providing attendees the opportunity to observe the first formation of two Eurfighters in flight. In contrast, during the 2002 Farnborough show, a flight formation of four aircraft starring DA1, DA2, DA4 and the IPA1 leading the formation, the latter already painted in gray air superiority were also presented for the first time and with historical character. .

In July 1998, the plane traveled to the Morón air base where it performed the environmental tests of extreme temperatures and whoever had the opportunity to spend a summer near Seville can understand what it means. Incidentally, Morón was the first base on which the Spanish Air Force deployed the aircraft operationally.

The environmental tests of DA6 continued at the base of Boscombe Down under the control of the DERA (Defense Establishment Research Agency), in which this British agency has a chamber for environmental control tests.

This hangar is suitably equipped to reproduce environmental conditions (temperature and humidity) from almost anywhere in the world and are the only ones of its kind large enough to house a full-fledged Eurofighter fighter aircraft. In this way, the plane can be safely and safely subjected to very realistic environmental conditions, before moving on to the flight experimentation phase.

The tunnel, equipped with a powerful fan, can simulate up to 350 knots of air velocity, while a combination of water and liquid nitrogen is introduced into the air stream to generate the desired freezing conditions.

From the month of November 1999 until the spring of 2000, the DA6 was subjected to temperatures of +/- 70ºC and extreme degrees of humidity, simulating the climatic conditions to which it will supposedly be exposed when they start operating around the world .

In order for a medical team to evaluate the physiological effects on the human body of these extreme conditions, several test pilots belonging to the four member nations of the consortium were chosen to take part in the trial. Dressed with full flight equipment were placed inside the cabin during the development of the trials, while the doctors monitored their vital signs.

In June of 1999 they had the opportunity to fly the plane in Getafe Lieutenant General Litzeracos, Chief of Staff of the Greek Air Force. This same month the first flight with the liquid cooling system of the crew was registered.

The next important guest in flying the DA6 would be Sir Robert Walmsey (UK CDP)

Another important testing phase carried out with the DA6, DA2 and DA4 is the implementation of the FCS 3R1 software for the FCS system, which corresponds to the production version for the initial operational capacity of serial production aircraft (SPA).

In March 2002 he was dedicated to testing the handling qualities in the subsonic regime and the Auto Low Speed Recovery subsystem (ALSR), plus tests of the DVI (Direct Voice Input), and Avionics and Systems for the two-seater. In October 2002, he was at the Morón air base (next to the DA1), to perform various flight tests; a month later it crashed in the province of Toledo, because the SW and DECU (Digital Engine Control Unit) caused a bad activation of the dynamic outlets of the motors, causing them to shut down. The pilots (Cuadrado and Lombo) were able to eject. It was temporarily replaced in Getafe by the DA1.

DA7: The last aircraft of the prototype lot is the DA7 and it is the second aircraft built by Alenia. It flew on January 27, 1997. Completing the puzzle of changing designations, we will say that this aircraft should have been the DA8. He was dedicated, as the DA3, to the tests of armament and separation of subalar charges. Received the registration MMX603

This aircraft was responsible for the first successful launch of a Sidewinder missile on the Decimomannu test site, followed in December 2001 by the supersonic launch to Mach 1.2 of another Sidenwinder. Given the long time required for the guided weapons work was concentrated on the AIM-9 and the AMRAAM in order to have them validated for the Initial Operational Capacity (IOC)

The launching of AMRAAM, carried out on May 17, 2000, did not imply the use of any target was only a test missile instrumented so that in the space dedicated to the war cargo was occupied by telemetry equipment. The missile, once launched from one of the ejection stations of the aircraft and after burning the fuel of the propeller engine, carried out a pre-programmed maneuver. This trial was followed by other AMRAAM tests in the Mach 1.6 supersonic regime. Also attributable to the DA7 is the firing of the first flares of the DASS system.

This prototype has made a valuable contribution to authorize the launch of the 1,000 liter tank flight, specially designed for the Eurofighter. The test was carried out successfully in July 1998, when a tank was launched at 1,504 m. (5,000 feet) altitude and at a speed of 684 km / h without problems. Currently the flight envelope has ex-

The IPA9 was delivered at the end of 2017, it is the SS 051 C.16-70 / 14-28, it belongs to the Air Force, it is dedicated to national and international tests: E-Scan radar, Meteor missile, etc. The 27 mm gun can be disassembled to install instrumentation for the aforementioned tests, FTI (Flight Test Instrumentation). [EA]

panded to Mach 2, the 9G and a maximum altitude of 16,765 m. (55,000 feet).

Currently all DAs have been withdrawn from use, and most are in museums.

The IPA

The Eurofighter production contract included a batch of three tandem planes and two instrumented single-seater aircraft, generically referred to as IPA (Instrumented Production Aircraft). The manufacture of the IPA belongs to the Production Contract. This is in force since January 30, 1998. Its duration is from this date until December 2018, if the additional options are included.

This contract, nicknamed "umbrella" (Production Investment + Series Production), involved the financing and delivery until 2015 of a total of 620 aircraft (original amount, which in 2011 was cut, while deliveries were extended until 2019), including five IPA (plus an extra one incorporated in 2018) to carry out tests and a PMAFT (Production Major Fatigue Test) batch. This contract was made up of a series of supplements.

The first one, Investment for Production (PI), was signed on January 30, 1998 (although it had an effect from January 1997) and ended in December 2005. Within this first supplement were the costs of the instrumentation (flight test instrumentation) and the operation of the IPA. All flight tests of the five IPAs were therefore covered by this contract, including those of IPA04, the first car, which was in the custody of EADS CASA (current Airbus Defense & Space).

The second first supplement of Serial Production (PS), entered into force from September 18, 1998, was therefore signed eight months later, and was valid until December 2005; then another one was signed with validity until 2019. In the original supplement is manufacturing, acceptance flights and activities associated with the first Tranche composed of 148 aircraft. This group was divided in turn into three batches, with the IPA included in the first.

Two-seater

IPA1: Built by BAE. Analysis of flight qualities, including airfreight and air-surface carefree handling, verification of structural loads, flutter tests in air-surface configuration and integration of weapons (CBLS200 / Paveway II and Meteor), DASS .

Status: Registration ZJ699. First flight made on April 15, 2002 from Warton with the pilot of the Eurofighter Project Keith Hartley and with the head of test pilots Paul Hopkins in the back seat. The flight lasted 26 minutes making the tracking flight (chase plane) a Tornado GR1 (ZA327). The next day the plane made its second flight. This was the first IPA (PT001) to start construction, so a series of small defects detected could be corrected during the initial phases of the construction of the following two IPAs. The first flight of the IPA1, was originally planned for August 2001, but was delayed due to a series of minor quality problems related to the component suppliers and the complexity of the aircraft. The truth is that Eurofighter officials were sincere and have admitted that "put 16,000 pieces together was somewhat complicated task."

IPA2: Built by Alenia. Analysis of actions in Air-Air and Air-Surface, Navigation tests and Landing Aids, integration of FLIR, "flutter" tests in Air-Air configuration and tank launch tests.

Status: Registration MMX614. First flight made on April 5, 2002 from the tracks of Turin / Caselle with Alenia's pilot test pilot, Commander Mauricio Cheli. The flight lasted 25 minutes. That same day, in the early afternoon, he undertook a second flight of engine testing and a third at the end of the day. This plane was the first of the IPA to fly.

IPA3: Built by EADS DASA. Analysis of the air-surface flight qualities, trials of ground actions, verification of the Flight Command System, including advanced functions of the Automatic Pilot, radar integration and Air-Air armament (AIM-9L / AIM-120B AMRAAM, AIM-2000 IRIS-T).

Status: Registration 98 + 03. First flight made on April 8 from the test flight center of the Wehrtechnische Diestselle 61 in Manching, with the pilot of the Eurofighter Program, Chris Worning and Luftwaffe Lt. Col. Robert Hierl, during the flight were accompanied by an F -4F (38 + 13), assigned to this experimental center. The duration of the flight was 31 minutes. This plane also made three flights on its first day. The second accompanied by a Tornado (46 + 10) and the third only.

Single-seaters

IPA4: Built by EADS-CASA (today Airbus Defnece & Space). Analysis of performances and flight qualities in Air-Air and Air-Surface configurations, including "carefree-handling" and "flutter" in the latter, Air-Surface weapon integration (GBU 10/16), environmental tests and MIDS verification , is PS001 C.16.20 / 11-91, it was retrofitted to Tranche 2 and later to 3A. There is also an ISPA (Instrumented Production Aircraft), which is the ST010 CE.16-10 / 11-79, lent to the industry, based on Getafe.

IPA5: Built by BAE. "Carefree handling" tests, verification of structural loads and operation of SHM (Structural Health Monitoring), integration of DASS and sensor fusion, fuel tests and weapon integration.

Status: Registration ZJ700. Since the Eurofighter program has not used a series of aircraft to go into mass production, as has been the case up to now, it may be interesting to clarify the differences between DAs, IPAs and serial aircraft.

The Airplanes of Development (DA), like all the prototypes, are airplanes "of the 80s", almost handmade and they have been used to refine the design. Many changes have been made to the cell, flight systems and mission systems, which have been subsequently incorporated into production aircraft. The aircraft instrumented as standard (IPA), have been built both in configuration and by the methods used, in the same way as the Aircraft Production Series (SPA) and incorporate the latest standards of equipment and technology, resulting much more reliable.

The only difference is that the necessary instrumentation for flight tests has been added to the IPAs. The same statement can be made with the engines. Those installed in the IPA are already series engines. The purpose of the IPA was to supplement the DAs in the final stretch of the Development Phase until achieving the Full Operational Capacity, in order to complete the verification of aircraft characteristics and their systems in a configuration identical to that of aircraft. of production and carry out the integration of specific weapon configurations of the series aircraft and not foreseen in the development prototypes. It is anticipated that a much lower volume of changes will result from your tests than those required for DAs.

In the areas where the IPA tests reveal the need to make more changes, and these, most likely, will consist in the refinement of the software, to optimize the performance of the weapons system and the sensors, rather than physical changes of the cell or flight systems.

IPA6 (United Kingdom) - Conversion of Series aircraft (BS031) - Phase 2 avionics systems.

IPA7 (Germany) - Conversion of Series aircraft (GS029) - Standard of Phase 2.

IPA8 - (Germany) First Typhoon with the E-Scan radar, integration of new armament and improvements in the mission team.

IPA9 - (Spain) Delivered at the end of 2017, it is the SS 051 C.16-70 / 14-28, belongs to the Spanish Air Force, is dedicated to national and international tests: E-Scan radar, Meteor missile, etc. The 27 mm gun can be disassembled to install instrumentation for the aforementioned tests, FTI (Flight Test Instrumentation).

The Typhoon of the future

Many have described the Eurofighter as a bridge to the FCAS (Future Combat Aircraft System) in which Germany and France are partners having recently joined Spain, but you can go further. The Eurofighter will also be at the core of the FCAS system, whatever it may be. Just look at the timeline, the Eurofighter will fly with the new fighter and within the FCAS system for more than 20 years.

And until a new fighter is developed, the Eurofighter will be the platform where some of the technologies that will be required for an FCAS will be tested and operationally implemented. We refer to connectivity, network weapons and remote operator, as well as manned / unmanned equipment. You just have to imagine in the time frame before an FCAS, that you could have an advanced Eurofighter flying with an unmanned system and that could dramatically increase the capacity of the aircraft in the theater of operations. It is a fantastic opportunity for Eurofighter because it can invest in greater capabilities and that would allow it to operate in the network environment of the future.

If the Eurofighter or the FCAS were made to fly in the future battle space environment, they will need large amounts of data. How are all these data taken to the theater from space or from command centers in Europe? You will need high speed and resistance to transmit all this information.

One possibility is laser communication. Airbus has a project called Network For The Sky that, among other technologies, is studying direct laser communication between satellites and airborne platforms, which provides a very high data rate combined with a strong and secure communication against interference. In addition, in another project, we are working on an intelligent tanker, that is, using an MRTT, flying just behind the tactical area, which can provide, through artificial intelligence, all the necessary data (instead of just fuel) to the fighter pilots in the theater of operations. These are the parameters of what FCAS will need.

It would also be investing money in directional data links to obtain own sovereign solutions.

Of course, the Eurofighter will comply with future communication standards and protocols that an FCAS will require.

The German Luftwaffe has definitively ruled out the F-35 (it has actually been the Ministry of Defense), and in the Tornado substitution program, the Boeing F/A-18E/F will compete and an advanced Eurofighter, equipped with many improvements, such as conformal tanks, with vector thrust nozzles, new large aerea cockpit display, etc. Spain also is interested in this advanced variante and at least half of the 40 additional Eurofighters to be purchased will be of this variant. [Eurofighter]

Possibly the future Eurofighter Typhoon Tranche 4 will be able to have important improvements in its equipment such as connectivity, network weapons and the remote operator, the crew/ unmanned systems. It just have to imagine in the time frame before an FCAS that it could have an advanced Eurofighter flying with an unmanned system and that could dramatically increase the capacity of the aircraft in the theater of operations. [Eurofighter]

In the development of new capabilities for the Eurofighter, the Instrumented Production Aircraft play an important role, among them the Spanish IPA4 (C.16-20 / 11-91) that we see here flying over the Gulf of Cádiz. [EA]

Tranches and updates of the spanish Typhoon

The Spanish Air Force received its first C.16 (ST001), in September 2003. In May 2004, the first three arrived in Morón, together with the crews who had completed the flight and maintenance courses in Getafe.

In 2012, a SS (single-seater) was received, leaving to deliver more than fifteen aircraft, but due to the critical economic situation that Spain was going through at the time, these Eurofighter as they left the Airbus facilities in Getafe, were stored in Los Llanos, in what he called "the corralito", (the little shed) being periodically flown so that his systems would work optimally. At the end of 2016 the Ministry of Defense paid the amount owed and the Typhoons were delivered in 2017 to the Air Force.

At the beginning of 2012 it was estimated that the delivery process would end in mid-2019, which has been met scrupulously with the delivery of C.16-76, -77 and -78.

Tranche 1

Spain has 17 Tranche 1 (T1), 10 SS (single-seater) and seven TS (two-seater) SI aircraft. On August 10, 2007, the last plane that completes the production of the T1 for the Air Force was received. They are all retrofitted to SRP (Service Release Proposal) 4.3 (PSC 3.31+) Production Software Configuration, although in some documents it appears as Production System Configuration), with the OFP01E tape, and the OFP02 will be implemented shortly, which among other improvements includes arriving to the T3A standard, including Meteor air-to-air missiles and GBU-48 dual pump (laser / GPS). There were 19, but it is necessary to discount the CE.16-08 that was crashed and the IPA 4 (C.16-20 / 11-91) that

The third Spanish two-seater in the final assembly phase at the facilities in Getafe of the then EADS CASA. [Airbus]

A CE.16 of Grupo 11 departing for a training mission, it is seen that it already bears the new fuselage numeral. [S. Mafé]

Hangar of the Ala 14 Maintenance Squadron. The C.16-68 carries the SRP (Service Release Proposal) 12 and the PSC (Production System Configuration) 12.23.40. [S. Mafé]

was retrofitted to the T2 (and later to the T3A) for tests of Industry. They are part of Batch 1 and 2 and Blocks 1, 1B, 1C. 2, 2B and 5.

With this final software and hardware version, the "FOCmax" capacity (full maximum operational capacity) in air-air configuration and complete in air-surface is considered achieved. With respect to previous Blocks the following improvements are included: Authorization of basic functionality of the MAW (Missile Approach Warner), improvements of interoperability of the MIDS (Multifunctional Information and Distribution System), improvement in the interoperability of radio channels at 8.33KHz, GPS and radar, introduction of the HEA (Head Equipment Assembly - pilot helmet with integrated viewfinder), and hardware obsolescence resolution, plus the integration of the Litening III pod

The serials of the T1 go from CE.16-01 to CE-16-07 and C.16-21 to C.16-30. In addition, we must also take into account the only Spanish prototype (DA6), registered XCE.16-01, which was lost in an accident in November 2002.

The Eurofighter has under the cockpit what is called the Maintenance Data Panel (MDP), which shows the general condition of the aircraft and its systems. [S. Mafé]

Tranche 2

The Air Force received a total of 34 aircraft (28 SS, six TS) including the SS021 (C.16-40), in exchange for the SS010 of the T1, which was delivered to Austria in December 2006. In addition the CE. 16-10 is an ISPA (Instrumented Series Production Aircraft). The SRP 12 is available and consists of three software versions: PSC 12.12.21, 12.12.31 and 12.23.40. Version similar to the SRP 4.3 of the T1, with improvements in automatic pilot, DASS (Defensive Aids Sub-System), pumps in the SFT (Supersonic Fuel Tank), radio, FLIR, Enhanced GPS and LARS (Launch Acceptable Region), is the "basket" for the GBU-10, GBU-16 and GBU-48 represented on the HUD. The S cor-

The C.16-57 / 11-27 is the last jet of the Tranche 2 received by the Air Force, corresponding to Block 11. [Pablo Gutiérrez Florido]

Two Typhoon Tranche 3 P1Eb (Phase 1 Enhanced Further Work) before being delivered to Ala 14. [Eurofighter]

In 2007 the Eurofighter Meet was held in Morón, in the photograph aircraft from the Spanish Air Force, the RAF and the AMI can be seen. [A. Machés]

Two Eurofighter of Tranche 1 armed with IRIS-T missiles flying over the Mediterranean Sea. [Eurofighter]

C.16-37 taking off from Los Llanos during a TLP Flying Course, this aircraft is currently in Ala 14 strengh. [Juanjo Fernández]

One of the eight two seat of Tranche 1, of which seven remain, since the CE.16-08 was lost in an accident. [Eurofighter]

responds to the plural, since there are several representations, according to the launching mode: LOFT, CCIP, etc. It should be LARs).

The improvement is being implemented, previously carrying the P1Eb FW (Phase 1 Enhanced Further Work) and now P2Eb (Phase 2 Enhanced Further Work) package that provides complete air-to-air and air-surface capacity, and includes, among other improvements, the following: laser designator pod (LDP) at station 0, Enhanced GBU-16 (GBU-48), Enhancement 1 to 3 DASS, IRIS-T missile Phase 2 (digital), radio channel spacing (8.33MHz) and IFF Mode 5 (interrogator and transponder). This improvement can be made in the bases themselves, and adds more functions, including the full integration of Meteor and it is expected that the Air Force has a squadron of 16 fully operational aircraft with this configuration.

The license plates of T2 are from CE.16-09, CE-16-13 plus CE.16-14 and C.16-31 to C.16-57. It will therefore be left unassigned the number-

Eurofighter Typhoon of Grupo 1 in the alarm shelter (QRA) of Morón. [Pablo Gutiérrez Florido]

Eurofighter Typhoon C.16-54 captured during a rainy day at the Morón air base. [Pablo Gutiérrez Florido]

ing from 13 to 19, since only 12 two-seaters were acquired. T2 is divided into Blocks 8, 8B, 9, 10, 11 and 15 and Batch 3.

Tranche 3

Spain should have received 34 airplanes, but with widespread cuts it stayed in 20 of the sub-variant Tranche 3A. Deliveries began in 2015. The improvements included are: integration of the AIM-120C5 / C7 AMRAAM, Meteor and Taurus missiles; integration of the SDB (Small

Rolling for takeoff on a night training flight. [Pablo Gutiérrez Florido]

Hangar of Grupo 11 Maintenance Squadron; it is perfectly appreciated that the Eurofighter in the foreground has just been applied the new numeral: 11-53, which corresponds to the same tail number, C.16-53; In this way the work of line personnel is greatly simplified. [S. Mafé]

During the 2018 Tiger Meet in Poland, the Spanish "Tiger" flew in formation with German and Italian tigers. [Eurofighter]

Spectacular image of a Eurofighter from Ala 14 in the QRA shelter at Los Llanos. A plane is maintained 24/7 in 15 minutes and another in an hour. [Jorge Portalés]

With the two EJ200 at full power the "14-24" starts its takeoff roll for a night flight. [S. Mafé]

The typical configuration of the Eurofighter in QRA is two IRIS-T "war" missiles, full ammunition for the 27 mm cannon and two fuel tanks with a capacity of 1,000 liters each, and which are supersonic, so they do not affect the performance of the plane. [S. Mafé]

Diameter Bomb) pumps and implementation of the improvements 4 and 5 of the DASS. The license plates of Tranche 3 go from C.16-60 to C.16-78, carry the Service Release Proposal 12 and the Production System Configuration12.23.40, all are from Batch 4 and Blocks 20 and 25. As a curiosity we will say that the T3A for Oman are Block 30 and the T-3B for Kuwait and Qatar Block 40.

In summary, the P2E capabilities package includes numerous novelties that represent a real milestone in the process of constant evolution of the Eurofighter. This package is provided in two increments P2Ea and P2Eb, which allows a more gradual incorporation of the improvements. At this moment, the Air Force is in the process of implementing the P2Eb, which includes all P2Ea improvements plus others available only in this second increment.

However, the plans of the Air Force contemplate the purchase of 40 additional Eurofighter, among which would be included 16 Tranche 3A, of which 14 would be to replace the exhausted F / A-18A Hornet of 462 Squadron of Gando, in the period 2023 -2025, two to cover the attrition of Wings 11 and 14 and the rest in an advanced version, something more than the Tranche 3B, and that would include EJ200 engines with greater power, reliability and vector thrust nozzles, plus conformable fuel tanks , these could replace the F-18M of Torrejón or Zaragoza, and would use some of the technologies developed for the future European combat aircraft called FCAS (Future Combat Aircraft System), that is why internally it is called Eurofighter pre-FCAS or Long Term Evolution. On the other hand, the Consolidated Package of the P3Eb will be implemented in the Spanish T2 and T3A in 2021, integrating the Brimstone New Design missile.

Initially the Air Force acquired twelve Litening III for the Eurofighter, but this year (2019) will receive another twelve, although of the most advanced version Litening III Gen.5. [S. Mafé]

Tranches and blocks	
Tranche 1	
Block 1:	Initial operational capacity (IOC for its acronym in English) and air defense capacity.
Block 2:	Initial air-air capacities.
Block 2B:	Complete air-air capabilities.
Block 5:	Complete operational capacity (FOC) standard combining existing air-air capabilities with air-ground capabilities. All Tranche 1 aircraft have been updated with the capabilities of Block 5 through the reconversion program called R2.
Despite some news to the contrary, the Tranche 1 aircraft can be converted to Tranche 2, it would be to change several processors and other elements (see below) and move a bulkhead slightly. However, it is possible that the Air Force does not undertake this update due to the cost involved, however with the SRP4.3 + and the OFP01E (the latter developed by CLAEX), its capacity as "swing-role" hunting is practically equal to T2.	
Tranche 2	
The Tranche 2 aircraft were in production until 2015. Although they carry the CAPTOR-M radar, they can be updated with the AESA CAPTOR-E Mk1 as well as the T3A, although the Air Force would choose a derivative thereof.	
Block 8 and 8B:	New mission computers (hardware) necessary for the integration of weapons such as the Meteor and Taurus missiles. Differences in construction with Tranche 1 related to obsolescence or changes in production technology.
Block 10:	Increased operational capacity (EOC) 1,
Air-to-air:	AIM-120C-5 AMRAAM, IRIS-T digital
Air-ground:	GBU-10/16/48.
Designator:	Rafael Litening III
Block 15:	EOC 2,
Air-air:	Meteor,
Air-land:	Taurus, Storm Shadow, Brimstone.
Tranche 3A	
Block 20/25:	EOC 3.
Similar to T2	

The spacious and modern cabin of the Eurofighter Typhoon. [S. Mafé]

Retrospective look at Morón, when the "shelter" had not yet been built, which has been proliferated by Spanish air bases. [S. Mafé]

The then Colonel Leon Antonio Machés Michavila, when he was the Commanding Officer of Ala 11 in 2007. [S. Mafé]

Brigadier General León Antonio Machés Michavila – Head of Air Systems AF. Subdirectorate General for Program Management. General Directorate of Armament and Material

He entered as a soldier in the Air Force in 1973. He belongs to the 32nd Promotion of the General Air Academy. He made the course of Hunting and Attack in the Reactors School of Talavera, passing destined to the Wing 21 of the Air Base of Morón with F-5 airplanes. During this period he completed Advanced Air Traffic Control (FAC) and air support courses. He was selected to take the "Fighter Weapons Instructor" course with the USAF at the famous Fighter Weapons School in Nellis AFB. Later it was destined to the wing 15 of new creation with the F-18 Hornet in the Aerial Base of Saragossa, where it remained until its ascent to the rank of commander. He took the General Staff course and at the end he went to the Operations Division of the Air Force Staff, where he was in charge of the first participation of the EA in the Red Flag exercise in 1994, in Nellis AFB. He was also in charge of the TLP, ACMI and TACEVAL exercises. He contributed to the operations in the former Yugoslavia, stationed at the Air Operations Center (AOC) in Kiselynk.

He went to the MOA and later to MACOM, destinations in which he participated actively in numerous exercises and operations, highlighting his performance several times as national representative in the CAOC of the 5th ATAF in Vicenza during operations on the Balkans.

He made the command of the Lieutenant Colonel in the 15th wing of Zaragoza as Head of the Material Group and later of the Air Force Group, during this period he acted as Tactical Commander and Head of the Detachment of the EA in the Air Base of Aviano (Italy) in three occasions, participating in all operations.

At the end of the command he was assigned to the NATO Agency, NETMA of the Eurofighter Program in Munich and subsequently to the MALOG / DIS Office of the EF2000 Program.

He was subsequently assigned to CLAEX, where he served as Chief of the Aeronautical Software Group and Head of the Flight Testing Group.

Lately he has participated in ISAF operations in Afghanistan as J4 in the EM of the RAC in Herat. On July 17, 2007, he was appointed Chief of Ala 11 and Morón Air Base, being in this position until September 2009, being assigned to MACOM as Head of Training, Exercises and Evaluation. In February 2010 he was appointed Head of the Herat base in the West Regional Command of the ISAF (Afghanistan). After returning to Spain he was assigned to the Logistics Command, Systems Management as Head of the Eurofighter Program Office. In January 2011 he was promoted to Brigadier General and spent three years as Division Leader Support at NETMA. After this destination, he was appointed Chief of the Logistics Division of the General Staff of the Air Force, in his General Headquarters in Madrid. In February 2015, he was transferred to the Ministry of Defense and appointed Head of Air Systems, General Subdirectorate for Program Management, of the General Directorate of Armament and Material. In this position he is responsible for programs such as Eurofighter, A400M, FCAS, ITS, UAS and others.

It has more than 3,500 hours of flight in jets.

Clarification to acronyms

TRANCHE: In Spanish section, means the different variants of Eurofighter, which in turn, according to software or updates are divided into Batches (Lots) and Blocks (Blocks) and within these are the SRP (Service Release Proposal as well as the PSC (Production System Configuration.
SS: Spanish Single (monoplace)
ST: Spanish Trainer (two-seater)
Complicated, right? Well, that's the Eurofighter Typhoon, a design in constant evolution, but if we look at the other side of the Atlantic Ocean, Boeing with its F/A-18E/F Super Hornet and EA-18G Growler, it does not gets so complicated.

The CLAEX

The CLAEX makes its first launch of an EGBU-16 bomb (also known as GBU-48) from a Eurofighter Typhoon
A test team from the Logistics Center of Armament and Experimentation of the Air Force (CLAEX) successfully carried out the first launch of an EGBU-16 (GBU-48) pump from a C.16 of Tranche 2.
The launch was carried out in the week of June 20 to 24, 2017, in the waters of the Gulf of Cádiz, and with the support of the 'El Arenosillo' experimentation center of CLAEX, after proceeding to the identification of the objective, to the guided launch by GPS signal and its laser illumination during the terminal phase by means of the new generation Litening III pod, installed in the central support of the C.16 launcher.
This event supposes the certification of a remarkable increase in the air-surface capacities of the C.16 fleet, allowing carrying out attacks 'all time' and of great precision in a totally autonomous way. Also, the weapon used will allow the C.16 to make simultaneous attacks on several land targets.
In conjunction with the evaluation of air-surface weapon integration, the first IRIS-T was also launched in digital mode, carried out from C.16 Tranche 2 and 3A aircraft. This will allow in the very near future to have this capacity in the complete Eurofighter fleet of the Air Force, after the integration carried out by CLAEX for Tranche 1 aircraft and verified in 2015, ahead of other users of the weapons system.
These achievements demonstrate the firm will of the Air Force to maximize the capabilities of the C.16 weapons system in the shortest possible time, advancing the entry into service of Tranche 2 aircraft with new capabilities developed through the international program and implementing in parallel organic developments in Tranche 1 aircraft.
Enviar comentarios

The maintenance personnel is essential so that the air force units have the necessary airplanes to fulfill their mission. [Jorge Portalés]

First mission with F-22 of the 95th Fighter Squadron, 325th Fighter Wing of the Eurofighter of Wing 14. In the C.16 of the bottom Captain Juarez. In the CE.16 that makes the photo Captain De los Pinos piloting the plane and Captain Arizaga in the rear cabin making the photo. The Eurofighter called Long Term Evolution, which will be the Tranche 4, will carry E-SCAN radar, more powerful engines with vector thrust nozzles, conformal tanks and the instrument panel will be a single touch screen, such as the F-35.

Typhoon "11-03", a Tranche 1 upgraded with the same software as the late Tranche two, takes off from Getafe airfield, after the upgrade was performed by Airbus. [EA]

Extraordinary photograph of a C.16 of the 14th wing, at the controls the captain Manuel Bermejo Casado; Captain Gregorio Serrano Arizaga, captured this image of the 40,000 pounds of thrust of the two engines EJ200 (In thrust we trust!)

Typhoon in action

Baptism BY FIRE: Odyssey Dawn and Unified Protector operations

Since March 19, 2011, Operation Odyssey Dawn began, the initial name of the implementation of Resolution 1973 of the UN Security Council, in order to protect Libyans from the excesses of Colonel Gaddafi and his regime. Typhoon FGR4 of the RAF (deployed in Gioia del Colle, southern Italy) and of the AMI -Aeronau-

Since March 19, 2011, Operation Odyssey Dawn began, the initial name of the implementation of Resolution 1973 of the UN Security Council. in order to protect Libyans from the excesses of Colonel Gaddafi and his regime, 4 RAF Typhoon FGR4s (deployed in Gioia del Colle, southern Italy) and AMI -Aeronautica Italiana-Militare (operating from Trapani in northern Sicily), the implementation of the Air Exclusion Zone began to contribute. On March 31, the leadership of the mission became the responsibility of NATO and changed its name to Operation Unified Protector. [Crown Copyright-MOD]

As the Islamic State has been expelled from most of the territory they once had, the Typhoon of the Royal Air Force (RAF) in the UK in Operation Shader are flying fewer missions planned attacks, and instead are increasingly used for armed "surveillance", with a greater emphasis on non-traditional intelligence, surveillance and recognition (ISR). [Crown Copyright-MOD]

NATO has been protecting the skies of the Baltic since 2004, when Estonia, Latvia and Lithuania joined the Alliance. The Baltic Air Policing mission began in April 2004 and has been continuously implemented since then. The airspace of Slovenia is covered by Hungary and Italy, while Albania and Montenegro are covered by Greece and Italy. All NATO member nations that possess an air surveillance capability contribute voluntarily to the NATO mission in the Baltic States and this responsibility is rotated every four months. The capacity for the mission in the Baltic States was established by the deployment of NATO warplanes to the Šiauliai Air Base in Lithuania. Since 2014, NATO has also been using the Amari AFB in Estonia for the deployment of additional assets. The Luftwaffe contributes regularly with its Eurofighter, despite the low operational availability of its fleet. [Luftwaffe]

Safeguarding the integrity of the sovereign airspace of the members of the Alliance is a task of peace that contributes to the collective defense of NATO. It is a clear sign of cohesion, shared responsibility and solidarity throughout the Alliance. The mission of NATO air police carried out using the Integrated Air and Missile Defense NATO (NATINAMDS) system, the F-2000A Eurofighter Italians have long collaborated on this mission. [Cristina Schrik]

A Eurofighter of the Aeronautica Militare Italiana making a maximum performance takeoff from the Air Base of Šiauliai, Lithuania. [AMI]

Eurofighter EF-2000 of the Luftwaffe in its 2shelter of alarm in Amari, Estonia. [Luftwaffe]

An EF-2000 intercepting a Beriev A-50 «Shmel», designation NATO Mainstay. Russian planes never make a flight plan and always carry the transponder off. [NATO]

tica Militare Italiana-, (operating from Trapani in the north of Sicily), began to contribute the implementation of the Air Exclusion Zone. On March 31, the leadership of the mission became the responsibility of NATO and changed its name to Operation Unified Protector.

But it was on April 12 when the RAF began to use its Typhoon as attack aircraft, it was a mission against several Gaddafist battle tanks. The pilot who participated in it said: "I took off from Gioa del Colle as part of a mixed section, with a Tornado GR4. We headed to Misrata, in western Libya, a city besieged by troops loyal to Gaddafi, where civilians were constantly attacked. It was an armed reconnaissance, in order to observe the main access routes. We detected a complex with about 10-15 tanks in its interior. We report the find to the command and control center, and we quickly receive authorization to attack.

At that moment, we generate the coordinates of the target and launch our weapons.

A Su-34 "Fullback", intercepted over the Baltic by Italian F-2000s. [NATO]

The Spanih Air Force has participated in five occasions in the BAP: Mirage F1M (Ala 14), Eurofighter (Ala 11, twice and Ala 14 twice with Typhoons) EF-18M (Ala 15) and in 2019 Ala 12 (EF -18M). [C.Schrik]

We always evaluated the possible effect that the weapon would have and if there was a possibility of collateral damage. It was a precision attack developed from considerable altitude (about 20,000 feet). To be honest, I was a little nervous, but in those moments one remembers the training that has been done before. He had thrown enough bombs from the Typhoon during numerous training missions. There was no difference with the real mission, only that at that moment I felt more relieved after checking the impact of the bomb, right where I had pointed it, through the image of the designator Litening III. We had proven that our fighter can carry weapons at a great distance, launch them with precision, land, refuel, reload weapons, leave for another mission, daily or several times during the same day, depending on operational requirements. We believe that our first mission was an important milestone in the "short-lived operational history of the Typhoon."

On the other hand the Wing Commander (Lieutenant Colonel) JJ Attridge, pilot of the RAF and head of the Typhoon detachment in Gioia de Colle, Italy, in Operation Ellamy, made the following comments about air operations.

"I carried out 30 sorties in support of Resolution 1973 of the United Nations Security Council, with an average duration of five hours, so I think I am qualified to say that the Typhoon has matured. In a little over three months we have flown almost 1,300 hours.

The deployment capacity and relevance of this new generation combat aviation has been amply demonstrated during the rapid deployment to the air base of Gioia del Colle, 72 hours after the implementation of the UN mandate, carrying out the first twelve missions hours later in Operation Odyssey Dawn.

However, more impressive has been the change of mission of the Typhoons and their pilots, from air superiority fighter to attack fighter bomber.

From the pilot's perspective, the plane is spectacular. Despite spending an average of seven hours in the mission cabin, it is not possible to find an airplane so comfortable to fly. The cockpit is large according to the standards of the combat aircraft and the information of the radar, DASS and Link 16 is shown in a simple and accessible way. This allows you to operate one hundred percent during each exit, without affecting fa-

An Ala 11 pilot in the cockpit of his Eurofighter ready for a scramble. [C. Schriek]

Spain contributed in 2018 with six Eurofighters of Ala 11 of Morón and a total of 131 people, being denominated to all the contingent "Detachment Vilkas". [C. Schrik[

tigue or lack of spatial attention. Due to the great power of its engines it is possible that the flight between Gioia and Libya, about 650 miles, lasts a little over an hour, at cruising speed, 0.9 mach and 40,000 feet, even with a military load of four bombs. 454 kg. Enhanced Paveway II, a Litening III designator pod, plus AMRAAM and ASRAAM missiles.

On the whole I have been very fortunate to be able to verify the maturation of the first really versatile combat aircraft of the RAF. We have also had the good fortune to have at our disposal an aircraft that satisfies the mantra of the RAF for agility, adaptability and capacity, as an American pilot told me: The Typhoon is a lot of everything for what it costs ". This assertion is confirmed by the following figures: the average number of hours flown by airplane during this operation has increased from 24 to almost 90 per month, which demonstrates the sensational availability of the platform.

Together with the GR4 Tornado, the Typhoon has enabled the United Kingdom to meet its commitment to the UN mandate in the so-called no-fly zone, while continuing to provide air defense in the United Kingdom and its dependencies. "

The Italian Eurofighters also took part in this operation, so F-2000A of the 4th and 37th Stormi were deployed to Trapani (Sicily), from where they were of QRA before carrying out aerial combat patrols in the no-fly zone over Libya and escort of the Tornado formations of the AMI in their attack missions.

Operation Shader

As the Islamic State has been expelled from most of the territory it once had, the Typhoons of the Royal Air Force (RAF) in the United Kingdom under Operation Shader are flying fewer planned attack missions, and instead they are using more and more for armed 'surveillance', with a greater emphasis on non-traditional intelligence, surveillance and recognition (ISR).

However, they fly armed with four 500 lb Raytheon Paveway IV bombs and these are used every time they locate and identify the Islamic State forces. However, as the Islamic State becomes an insurgency, the Typhoon pilots regularly use the Litening III laser designation pods of the aircraft as an ISR sensor.

Dedicated ISR platforms compile an intelligence image over time to obtain an understanding of the normal pattern of the area of operations and Typhoons are used to build that image, trying to find specific intelligence about individuals, groups and networks. The pod Litening incorporates the improved remotely operated video receiver (ROVER), which allows ground forces to see the same image as the pilot and share the same awareness of the situation.

In addition to being used to ensure the separation of other aircraft and the airspace deconcentrator, the Euroradar Captor-M radar of the aircraft can be used for air-surface tracking.

When the operation is aimed at clearing fighters of the Islamic State from their remaining stronghold, some villages in the Middle Valley of the Euphrates River (known as MERV), air strikes are expected to be more frequent again. By then, the Typhoon is deploying a new weapon in the form of MBDA Brimstone 2, which currently carries the Tornado GR4. The Tornado was scheduled to retire from Operation Shader in February, before leaving RAF service in March, and the Tornado's weapons capabilities (including the MBDA Storm Shadow cruise missile) are migrating to the Typhoon under the Centurion program. three phases. All these innovations were incorporated at the end of 2018.

Eurofighter Typhoon of Ala 14 in the BAP, is armed with AIM-2000 IRIS-T and AIM-120B AMRAAM missiles. [Ala 14]

Group photograph duien the accomplishment of the 400 flight hours carried out by the detachment of Ala 14. [EA]

The Ala 14 detachment operated during the first months of 2016. The photograph shows a C.16 ready for a training mission, as it is seen that it does not carry weapons. [Ala 14]

Baltic Air Policing

Safeguarding the integrity of the sovereign airspace of the members of the Alliance is a task of peace that contributes to the collective defense of NATO. It is a clear sign of cohesion, shared responsibility and solidarity throughout the Alliance.

The NATO mission of the Air Police is carried out using the NATO Integrated Air Defense and Missile System (NATINAMDS).

The Supreme Allied Commander of Europe (SACEUR) has the overall responsibility to carry out the NATO Police mission.

The Allied Air Command (AIRCOM) based in Ramstein, Germany, oversees the NATO Air Police mission with command and control 24 hours a day, seven days a week, from two Combined Air Operations Centers (CAOC)); one in Torrejón, Spain, and one in Uedem, Germany. CAOC Uedem is responsible for the NATO Air Police north of the Alps and CAJ Torrejon for the south. The CAOC decides which intercepting aircraft will receive the scramble order (ie, in charge of reacting) according to the location of the incident.

It is usual during these detachments to carry out exercises with the air forces of nearby countries, and of those that are also deployed, as it is the case of these Swedish Saab J39Cs and French Mirage 2000-5Fs. [NATO]

It was in the rotation of 2018 when a C.16 accidentally fired an AIM-120B AMRAAM during an air combat mission dissimilar with French Mirage 2000-5F, fortunately the self-destruct system worked and the deadly missile did not reach the fighter of the Armée de l'Air. [NATO]

Two Sukhoi Su-27 "Flanker" intercepted by Typhoon of Ala 14. [Ala 14]

The member nations of NATO provide the aircraft and the necessary assets for aerial surveillance of their own airspace, under the direction of SACEUR. Those who do not have the necessary means to do so (Albania, Estonia, Latvia, Lithuania, Montenegro and Slovenia) receive assistance from other NATO members to preserve the integrity of their sovereign airspace in times of peace and guarantee their security.

NATO has been protecting the skies of the Baltic since 2004, when Estonia, Latvia and Lithuania joined the Alliance. The Baltic Air Policing mission began in April 2004 and has been continuously implemented since then. The airspace of Slovenia is covered by Hungary and Italy, while Albania and Montenegro are covered by Greece and Italy.

All NATO member nations that possess an air surveillance capability contribute voluntarily to the NATO mission in the Baltic States and this responsibility is rotated every four months. The capacity for the mission in the Baltic States was established by the deployment of NATO warplanes to the Šiauliai Air Base in Lithuania. Since 2014, NATO has also been using the Amari AFB in Estonia for the deployment of additional assets.

The mission of patrolling the skies along the eastern border of NATO intensified in 2014 after the start of the Russia-Ukraine crisis.

Spanish Leadership within the NATO's Baltic Air Policing mission comes to and end

Šiauliai (Lituania)

14th Wing ‚Eurofighters' have been handed over by Danish and Portuguese F-16's, which will lead the Quick Reaction Alert mission as part of the Air Police in the Baltic

The Baltic Air Policing mission aims at guaranteeing and preserving the collective allied defence within the airspace of the Baltic republics as NATO member states, as well as the inviolability of their skies.

Spain has led from April 30 to August 31 the Baltic Air Policing mission „BAP", deploying seven ‚Eurofighter', four of which were transferred to NATO's chain of command.

BAP handover/takeover (HOTO) ceremony has taken place at Šiauliai air base observing all COVID-19 health protocols and with limited duration and reduced personnel attendance.

Colonel Dainius Guzas, Head of the Lithuanian Air Force, opened the ceremony addressing some words of acknowledgement and appreciation to the Spanish contingent for the excellent work carried out. In his speech, he wished the same success to the Danish and Portuguese contingents that will be part of the BAP-57. Afterwards he awarded with the BAP medal to representatives of the Spanish detachment. During the ceremony, the Spanish Force Commander, Lieutenant Colonel Bayardo Abós Álvarez-Buiza, presented the Danish and Portuguese Force Commanders the symbolic key to the Baltic countries' airspace.

Baltic Air Policing is a peacetime mission undertaken on a rotational basis by NATO member countries.

The incorporation of Latvia, Lithuania and Estonia to NATO in 2004 marked the extension of allied airspace to the north-east. Allied countries provide the Baltic republics with the necessary support to enable them to monitor and control their territory, conducting Quick Rapid Alert (QRA) missions.

Spanish ‚Eurofighters', along with four Italian F-35's at Ämari air base (Estonia), have been tasked with intercepting and identifying civilian or military aircraft that do not comply with international flight regulations, which approach into allied airspace or which have not been properly identified by air traffic control systems.

"Vilkas 2021" detachment, was made up of 134 military personnel (including a 28 airmen relief) deployed in Lithuania at the Šiauliai air base and in the town of Karmėlava.

Baltic Air Policing is a mission that has been carried out continuously since 2004, 365 days a year, 24 hours a day. Spain has taken part in the mission since 2006, on eight occasions. During this rotation the detachment has conducted over 750 flying hours, carrying out a total of 417 take offs and 211 missions, including 28 ‚alfa scramble' interceptions and identifications.

The Spanish Air Force in the Baltic Air Policing operation

Spain contributed in 2018 with six Eurofighter of Ala 11 of Morón and a total of 131 people, being denominated to all the contingent "Detachment Vilkas", it was in this rotation when a C.16 accidentally shot an AIM-120B AMRAAM during on a dissimilar air combat mission with French Armée de l'Air Mirage 2000-5Fs, fortunately the system of self-destruction worked and the deadly missile did not reach the Armée de l'Air fighter.

It was the fifth time that Spain participated in the BAP, after deploying Mirage F1M in 2006, Eurofighter sin 2015 (Ala 11) and 2016 (Ala 14) and EF-18M (Ala 15) in 2017 and EF-18M (Ala 12) in 2019.

Together with Portugal, which led the mission from Siauliai and France, which operated from the Ämari Air Base in Estonia, this was the 47th rotation of the BAP mission.

On September 1, 2018, the witness was handed over to Belgium and Germany.

Deployments of Wing 11

Estonia:

from December 2014 to May 2015.

Aircraft: C-16-40, 43, 46, 51

Flight hours: 446.

Lithuania:

from April 2018 to September 2018.

Aircraft: C.16-33, 40, 51, 54, 57, 63.

Flight hours: 1,016.

Deployments of Wing 14

1st Detachment (Mirage F1M): August 1 to November 30, 2006

2nd Detachment (Eurofighter): January 5 to May 1, 2016

The Spanish Force Commander, Lieutenant Colonel Bayardo Abós Álvarez-Buiza, presented the Danish and Portuguese Force Commanders the symbolic key to the Baltic countries' airspace, during the turnover in September 2021. [Ala 14]

Vilkas 2021 badge. [Ala 14]

Poster of the Vilkas Detachment in the hangar of the Maintenance Squadron of Grupo 11 of Morón. [S. Mafé]

Vilkas Detachment 2018.

RAF Typhoons scrambled twice in one day to intercept Russian military aircraft

Royal Air Force (RAF) Typhoon fighter jets operating from Ämari Air Base in Estonia launched twice on Tuesday 25th June to intercept Russian military aircraft flying close to Estonian airspace.

Typhoons first intercepted a Russian military transport aircraft before later intercepting two Russian Flanker fighters and another military transport aircraft.

This is a routine mission for the Typhoons conducting NATO enhanced Air Policing, providing reassurance that the UK is working in partnership with Estonia.

The contacts on both scrambles flew safely and operated in a professional manner throughout the intercept.

A Typhoon pilot from XI(Fighter) Squadron, attached to 121 Expeditionary Air Wing (EAW), who was conducting Quick Reaction Alert (QRA) duty when the first scramble was called said:

"We were scrambled to intercept a single aircraft that was flying down the Finnish/Estonian border from the East. We were tasked to identify the contact and shadow which is standard protocol.

"We identified the contact as an AN-12 (Cub) military transport and shadowed it in a westerly direction. Once the task was completed we were cleared to leave the contact and conduct training in segregated Estonian airspace."

On the second scramble, one of the Typhoon pilots commented:

"We were scrambled to intercept three contacts that were transiting from north west Russia around Estonia to Kaliningrad. We were tasked to identify the contacts and shadow them.

"We intercepted the aircraft off the west coast of Estonia, identified the contacts as an IL-22 (Coot B) military transport and two SU-27 Flanker fighters. The contacts were shadowed southward before handing them over to Swedish Quick Reaction Alert aircraft, two SAAB Gripens."

The Royal Air Force is deployed on Operation AZOTIZE in Estonia in support of Baltic Air Policing. This is the tenth and eleventh QRA scramble and intercept respectively since the RAF took over enhanced Air Policing (eAP) from the German Air Force on 3 May 2019 as part of Baltic Air Policing.

The UK operates in support of NATO to reassure our allies and is a further demonstration of the UK's commitment to the security of the region.

RAF Typhoons intercepting Russian aircraft, June 2019. [Crown copyright/MOD]

Image of a Grupo 11 Typhoon flying over the vicinity of the Morón air base; it is appreciated that it has the Litening III pod on the centerline station. [JM Martínez Morales]

Single-seater and two-seater of Ala 11 captured during a training flight [Geoff Lee / Eurofighter]

Single-seater and two-seater of Ala 11 captured during a training flight [Geoff Lee / Eurofighter]

The Typhoon in the Spanish Air Force

Grupo 11, Ala No. 11

Just over fifteen years ago, 113 Squadron was formed, one of the three with which Grupo 11 of Ala No. 11 of the Seville air base of Morón should have.

In the Official Defense Bulletin number 11 of January 19, 2004, Instruction number 175/2003, of December 23, of the Chief of Staff of the Air Force, General Eduardo González Gallarza-Morales, was published when 113 Squadron (call-sign "GALLO") of Air Forces was created.

Once the reception of the first C.16s (Eurofighter) by Grupo 11 (under the command of Lieutenant Colonel Juanas) of Ala 11 began, and in order to facilitate the destination and training of personnel who began to operate this weapons system , it was necessary to proceed to restructure the wing, in order to advance, as far as possible, the fate and instruction of the pilots who would operate it. This measure, contained in the "Implementation Plan for the C.16 Weapons System", aimed to reduce the effort that the operational squads should devote to the area of instruction at the time.

Thus, Grupo 11 of Ala 11 was restructured, being formed

by the following Squadrons:

- 111 Squadron.
- 112 Squadron. (not activated yet)
- 113 Squadron.

Grupo 11: At the end of 2018 it had 38 Typhoon on strengh, broken down as follows: Tranche 1: there are 17. (01, 02, 03, 04, 05, 06, 07, 21, 22, 23, 24, 25, 26, 27, 28, 29, 30).

Tranche 2: there are 19 (09, 13, 14, 32, 33, 35, 38, 40, 41, 42, 43, 46, 51, 52, 53, 54, 55, 57, 63).

Besides in 2019 was received C.16-56 a Tranche 2.

The aircraft CE.16-10 is assigned to Airbus and will be integrated into Grupo 11 in the future. As for the tactical numbers (fuselage numerals) General Instruction IG70-21 that was updated in July 2018, which orders the change of the numerals, which in Group 11 is made when each aircraft goes into maintenance and trying to start with the jets with the highest tail number, to avoid having two aircraft with the same number, which would be the case with the Tranche 1 between single-seaters with old numbers (Ex: C.16-21 (11-01) and two-seater with new numbering (Ex: CE.16-01 (11-01)), so when it is the turn of the two-seater, all the jets will be painted.

Grupo 11 has a staff of 19 pilots posted in both squadrons. This is due to the height of the crisis in 2008/2010 when the Ministry of Defense decided that the most experienced pilots (mainly captains with greater seniority, were posted to places not related to the flight, and since then it has not recovered, although it is expected to take measures to alleviate this deficit, which is quite serious for the whole national defense).

111 Squadron (call sign "DOLLAR") is committed to air defense and attack, although initially, the mission of the 111 Squadron was the operative evaluation of the Typhoon as a weapon system, including its armament, the writing of the documentation / operational manuals and of tactics.

In 2019 the 112 Squadron is still not activated due to the acute lack of pilots that the Air Force suffers as a whole.

To reach the maximum qualification (Package Lead) the pilot needs approximately 500 flight hours and have achieved the previous qualifications , which entails an approximate term of four years. The CR3 qualification could be obtained in less than two years, making the corresponding Basic Training Plans. Currently, the annual schedule of flight hours for a pilot of C.16 are 140 hours of flight plus 40 hours of simulator. However, a pilot can do more simulator hours, but never in exchange for flight hours. [Jorge Portales]

The 113 Squadron has, as a generic mission, the instruction of the pilots of the Air Force units equipped with C.16, that is, it is the Spanish Operation Conversion Unit for this combat aircraft.

The instruction to be given by the 113 Squadron is specified as follows:

- Pilot training without experience in Typhoon, up to Obtaining the qualification of Limited Combat Capacity (LCR, Limited Combat Ready).

The instruction of pilots who, having had the qualification of Combat Capacity (CR, Combat Ready) or Capacity Combat Limited (LCR, Limited Combat Ready), in said material, they have lost it and must recover it.

- Provide courses for flight instructor.

Captured with great skill by the camera of Juanjo Fernández, we see a Eurofighter from Ala 11 landing in Los Llanos during a TLP.

- Maintain Combat Capacity rating level 3 (CR-3, Combat Ready 3), of the instructor pilots.

In addition, the Personnel Command modified the postings and took appropriate measures to cover the aforementioned template. This Instruction came into force the day after its publication in the Defense Bulletin, so that date can be considered as the creation of the 113 Squadron.

On the other hand, the 111 Squadron was reactivated in October 2003, receiving its full operational capacity (FOC) in July 2008, when it began to perform the alarm service (QRA).

Morón Air Base

Morón was the base chosen by the Air Force to host the first operational squadrons of this new weapon system and the initial candidate to carry out the operational conversion of crews and ground personnel that equips the first line squadrons. Twenty-four kilometers of perimeter, more than 2,500 hectares of surface, a parking lot capable of parking 40 B-52 and a track of the longest in Europe (11,800x200 feet), endorse this decision and give this base the potential to host the infrastructures of the most complex weapons system. Its benign weather and a little conflictive airspace, with extensive training zones only ten minutes away, on water, act as multiplying factors in the performance of operations. Its geographic location is strategically adequate to allow immediate access to the area of the Strait, south of the Peninsula and the Canary Islands. Its local environment lacks large concentrations of population that can significantly restrict flight operations, and the base's roots in nearby towns is solid, cordial and positive as a result of a long and consolidated relationship. Since 1996, this base has housed F / A-18A aircraft from the CX program of the Air Force. Twenty-four second-hand units were acquired from the surplus of the US Navy, equipped with new engines. The last two planes scheduled to pass this revision were sent to the United States in direct flight by personnel from Ala 11 in August 2002 and were returned to Ala 46 at the beginning of 2003, along with the rest of the existing fleet in Morón that was transferred to the Canary Islands before the end of 2002, to leave room for the new tenant known internationally as Eurofighter Typhoon. Since the arrival of the F/A-18A, "CX", at the time Ala 21, was

To be an instructor of 113 Squadron there are a series of theoretical lectures where the instructor is instructed, where the particular objectives for each student are explained, in the flight they are variable, they include several rear cockpits, about seven flights to obtain the initial instructor qualification, then it is variable, depending on what the student knows, an instructor with a certain qualification is chosen. [Ala 11]

To be an instructor of 113 Squadron there are a series of theoretical lectures where the instructor is instructed, where the particular objectives for each student are explained, in the flight they are variable, they include several rear cockpits, about seven flights to obtain the initial instructor qualification, then it is variable, depending on what the student knows, an instructor with a certain qualification is chosen. [Ala 11]

The 111 Squadron, may be the most veteran fighter unit of the Air Force, originally activated (with another designation) at the Manises air base in 1955. Since then it has operated F-86F Sabre, Mirage IIIEE/DE , Mirage F1CE/EDA/DDA, F/A-18A and finally Eurofighter Typhoon. [S. Mafé]

Overview of the alarm barracks (QRA) of Morón, with an airplane in 15 minutes, another one hour and a third as a reserve. [S. Mafé]

Close-up of a Eurofighter piloted by Captain Joaquín Ducay. [Ala 11]

entrusted with the Air-Air mission and had been an integral part during these years of the Defense alert device, in addition to actively intervening in national and foreign exercises and maneuvers. They were an essential part in the crises associated with September 11, the Summit of European Heads of State or that of the Perejil Island. On July 30, 1999 and coinciding with the closure of the Manises Air Base, Morón went on to inherit the badge and history of Ala 11, Ala 21 la disappeared and was soon designated as a candidate to receive the first Eurofighter. A progressive plan was designed that contemplated the transfer of the Hornet aircraft to the Ala 46, in Gando (Gran Canaria) and that ended at the end of December 2002. During the year 2003, the unit concentrated on the instruction of its personnel and the preparation of the necessary infrastructures while waiting for the new aircraft in 2004.

Receiving a new weapons system is always a challenge, but the starting point of Wing 11

Lieutenant Colonel Manuel Maximiliano García de Veas is the Commanding Officer of Grupo 11, to his credit has 3,600 flight hours in jet aircraft, has been in the following destinations: Ala 2323 (Instructor F-5), Ala 14 (Mirage F1), Air Academy (Instructor C-101Aviojet), ENJJPT (Instructor T-38), MACOM (General Staff), Ala 11 (Eurofighter). He has participated in the following missions: ISAF and BAP (Captain with Mirage F1 and Lieutenant Colonel with Eurofighter). Graduated of the General Staff. Master in the University of Madrid in Defense Policy and International Security. [Jorge Portalés]

Beautiful image of a Eurofighter in his shelter at the Morón air base. [José Figueredo López]

The QRA reserve aircraft, photographed on November 28, 2018, is C.16-57 / 11-57, it is the last Tranche 2 single-seater received by the Air Force, and it carries the new numerals of fuselage. [Jorge Portalés]

Two pilots of Grupo 11; before debriefing, they pass through the Aircraft Generation Squadron, to sign the airplane book and report any discrepancies. These fascinating planes would not fly, nor could their skilled pilots carry out their complex missions, without the sacrificial effort of the maintenance personnel. [S. Mafé]

was solid and more favorable than that of other European partners in the program, since Morón must have adapted its personnel and structures from the F / A- 18 to a new airplane that supposed an evolution in terms of associated procedures and technologies. The case of Italy with the F-104 Starfighter, Germany with the F-4F Phantom and MiG-29 Fulcrum and Great Britain with its Tornado F3 ADV, was closer to a conceptual revolution as it was in its day for Spain the arrival of the F-18.

Ala 14 started operating its Eurofighter Typhoons since April 30, 2012, being shared with the veteran Mirage F1M, for about a year. [Ala 14]

Ala 14 has two assigned two-seaters, CE.16-11 / 14-70 and CE.16-12 / 14-71. [Ala 14]

Training

The Eurofighter training system differs from traditional systems by the exhaustive use of computer aids and aids in combination with an advanced didactic system that allows the controlled progress of each of the students, adapting to different levels of experience and any specialty with minimum requirements of personnel dedicated to instruction.

The manuals of the airplane, are computer programs of easy access, intuitive navigation and simple and attractive presentation, designed to run from a commercial PC. Its updating can be done with the ease and speed of replicating a DVD-type support, which only presents problems associated with the control of information or configuration control of the multiple existing publications.

The initial training of key personnel and pilots was carried out by the EADS-CASA industries (responsible for the cell and equipment) and ITP (responsible for the engine) in Getafe during 2003-2004. An initial group of 14 pilots, with experience in F-18 or Mirage F1 was designated for their instruction divided into three groups for their progressive incorporation to Morón with the arrival of the first aircraft. They were responsible for adapting the training plan on theorics and in flight prepared by the industry to the specificities of the Spanish air force; to build with their experience the tactical manuals of the aircraft and the best use of their equipment and systems: those in charge of designing and filling each of the missions of the training plan for a new pilot, during the seven months of their training alternating theoretical instruction, simulators and flight.

A section of Typhoon with pilots of the 142 Squadron at the controls. [Ala 14]

Pilot and crew chief talking after a mission [Tony García]

Lieutenant Colonel Pascual Soria Martínez is the current C.O. the Flying Operations Group of Ala 14. He entered the General Air Academy in September 1988, completing his training during the 5th year in the Fast Jet School (Ala 23). He was promoted to lieutenant in July 1993, his first posting being to Ala 14 (Albacete), where he would continue as Captain. [S. Mafé]

Since the beginning of 2019 a captain and a lieutenant of the Luftwaffe are taking the Eurofighter course at the Morón Air Base (Seville), with 113 Squadron. These are two officers with no previous fighter experience who have completed the jet course in the US.

All the phases are preceded by a number of theoretical lectures and practices in simulators, which are interspersed with the flights that are carried out both in tandem and in single-seater. The latter only on flights known as ‘loose’.

The course is divided into two plans. During plan 1 the pilots become familiar with the basic

The current Major José Navia-Osorio Torres was Ala 14 display pilot in 2017/2018. [Jorge Portalés]

With the EJ200 at full power, the Eurofighter barely needs 300 meters to take off. [S. Mafé]

This aircraft from Ala 14 carries SRP 12 and PSC 12.23.40. [S. Mafé]

management of the fighter. In plan 2 they do it with the management of the fighter in air-to-air combat scenarios, training with and against different platforms in a great variety of areas. Then the air-ground phase is performed, in which the pilots receive an approach to the handling of the aircraft in ground attack missions. In this phase, the pilots exercise the use of the C.16 cannon, an opportunity offered by the Bardenas range.

Once passed the plan 1 the pilots receive the qualification CA (with aptitude) and the card of instrumental flight, which allows them to fly alone in the airplane, adhering to some restrictions of operative and meteorological character.

With the completion of the course the new combat pilots in material C.16 acquire the LCR (Limited Combat Ready), which is the starting point in their new destinations, in a squadron equipped with this weapon system (111, 141 or 142).

This is the second course of the year (2018/2019), in which the participation of German pilots is included.

In Ala 14, LCR Pilots (Limited Combat Ready) make QRA, while in Ala 11, they do not have an internal operative instruction that perfectly defines the criteria and training that the pilot has to receive to make QRA.

Also in Grupo 11 there is internal operational instruction to move from wingman to section leader, and then to four-ship leader, to joint leader and finally to mission leader.

In Morón, when a new pilot arrives at the 111 Squadron he/she is LCR, and it can not do QRA until has received CR1 (Combat Ready 1) status, and in that process he/she is given an instruction with specific missions to make QRA, being assigned an instructor who advises which manuals have to be read, which national and NATO documentation has to be read, afterwards being examined.

A pilot who comes new to the 111 Squadron is wingman and to become a leader of a couple he is assigned a Plan 3 instructor and he/she is evaluated

Plan 1: Learn to fly the plane (in 113 Squadron)

Plan 2: Learn to fight basically with the plane (in 113 Squadron)

Plan 3: Extensive tactical part (111 Squadron)

During the P3 instruction, what a pilot needs to know to be a leader of a couple is defined:

- How many flight hours the pilot must have.
- How much experience in this type of mission.
- Finally the evaluation is done: it is several weeks and several flights, he/she have to plan the mission and carry it out under supervision.

142 Squadron returned with style to the Tiger Meet, it was at the Zaragoza air base in 2016, and it was clearly indicated in the drawing of the chosen aircraft, "14-06", we are back!. [Jorge Portalés]

In Grupo 11, the Eurofighter's 80% air-to-air operational tactics manual has been made in Spain. In principle, when C/CE.16 started, this manual was based on F-18 tactics. It is currently being revised to adapt it to the new MBDA Meteor missile, which is a worldwide revolution in aerial combat.

In Morón they took the very outdated manuals of the F-18 to make interceptions, in case the adversary fired before, and modified and updated them in full. That is, tables of Russian missile manuals, checking their ranges, distance tables, mnemonic rules, obtain formulas to serve as a generic rule to know when they have to start the maneuver and thus stay out of range of the missile.

Currently the tactics section has to develop:

- Combat with the Meteor

- Combat against radars over 90 ° sweep: A / C is now fought and when a missile is fired and is being supported before it enters active, it has to go towards the threat; With the new radars you can move away from the threat and withstanding the missile at the same time.

Maintenance Squadron Group 11

Maintenance is carried out daily on C.16, before each flight and after each flight.

It has maintenance stops every 25, 50, 100, 200, 400, 500, 800, 1000 flight hours and their respective multiples.

It has compliances by calendar of elements with useful life such as, for example, the para-

For the Tiger Meet of 2018 that took place in Poland 142 Squadron participated with another Eurofighter, the tail fin paint scheme was slightly different. [Eurofighter]

Each time a weapon capacity is incorporated, it usually involves a small software modification or even physical elements that will allow to incorporate these capabilities. They are currently being modified to incorporate the Meteor.

ALA 14

It has been more than six years since in June 23, 2013 was officially retired in Ala 14 the legendary Mirage F1 (aka: "the grandmother"), to make way for the Eurofighter Typhoon.

By 2020, by 2020 will have two wings equipped with this advanced 4+ generation fighter aircraft, Ala 11 (with squadrons 111, 112 -it will be activated if the pilot shortage is solved) and 113 - the latter the school of Typhoon of the EA- at Morón (Seville) and Ala 14 (Squadrons 141 and 142) of Los Llanos (Albacete). Since May 2011, the pilots of the 142 Squadron -as well as specialists and other technical branches- began the conversion process , arriving the first four planes to Los Llanos on April 30, 2012. Initially as a detachment of Ala 11, but in less than a year had its own entity, with numerals of Ala 14 and the badge of the same applied in the twelve Eurofighter Typhoon Tranche 2 PSC 3.70/3.78, which had been increased to 17 aircraft by mid-2016, including two two-seaters (CE.16) On September 1, 2017, 141 Squadron was re-activated (radio call sign "CHICO", 142 is "DARDO"), after receiving more planes, with which the Ala 14 again had two squadrons, with a fleet of 11 C.16 Tranche 2, two CE.16 T2 and 15 C.16 T3A; the last two Typhoons, C.16-77 and C.16-78 were received in the Spring of 2019. At the end of 2018 C.16-76 was received, while it must be taken into account that C.16-70 /14-28 is the IPA9, and the C.16-69 was destroyed on October 12, 2017, his pilot died, Captain Borja Aybar, with which are the Tranche 3A, delivered until 2019 to the Air Force, and a staff of 16 pilots assigned to both squadrons, plus four aggregated.

December 4, 2018, the Eurofighter in "QRA 15", is activated, but finally the mission is entrusted to a pair of Grupo 11 jets. [S.Mafé]

chutes and the cartridges of ejection elements such as the top and the seats.

It has compliances for "events", which are the number of times a system is activated. As for example the cooling system of the guidance head of the infrared missiles.

It has modifications in service issued by the manufacturer and sanctioned by the control that are incorporated to correct possible defects of the original design.

Apart it has its faults that it brings after flying and it is repaired daily.

Recurring hardware and software updates that affect avionics are incorporated.

Captain Fernando Caballero de Pro, from 142 Squadron, an experienced fighter pilot, who was also a pilot of "the grandmother" (the nickname of the Mirage F1M. [Jorge Portalés]

Comparing the Mirage F1M versus the Eurofighter Typhoon

Regarding the comparison between the Eurofighter and the Mirage F1, we bring to our pages the story of Captain (currently Major) Álvaro José Navia-Osorio Torres, pilot of the 142 Squadron (which was also display pilot during 2017-2018):

"The first obvious difference is found at the time of dressing, since the C.16 has its own flight equipment, much more complete, with a flight jacket (which incorporates a system of retention of arms at the time of ejection and part of the oxygen / communications system), an anti-g that covers the entire leg and waist and a helmet with an anti-g membrane on the nape of the neck (it becomes strange the first time you are inflated in flight).

Once equipped, we proceed to review the plane's book and see the possible discrepancies and shortcomings of the plane. When you get to the plane for the first time you can notice the difference in size and height compared to F1. The

Major Fernando Caballero de Pro of the 142 Squadron, posing in full flight gear, next to "QRA 15", December 4, 2018. At present time he is the C.O. of 141 Escuadrón. [S. Mafé]

Captain Juan Bengoechea (left) and Gregorio Serrano Arizaga, both of the 142 Squadron, this last is the current Ala 14 display pilot. [Jorge Portalés]

The Air Force (nor the rest of the Armed Forces), could not function properly without the valuable assistance of the non-commissioned officers. [Jorge Portalés]

The C.16 of Ala 14 in "QRA 15" photographed in a cold night in La Mancha. [Jorge Portalés]

exterior inspection is like any other plane, but it is appreciated not having to bend too much when checking the belly and train of the plane. Another very nice difference is the review of the captive armament, where we find the new IRIS-T instead of the AIM-9 (really is a radical change at the time of visual combat providing a great infrared superiority thanks to its seeker and maneuverability). When you get on the plane you realize how big and tall it is, since without a special ladder, getting on with the equipment is not an easy task.

Once tied and connected to the seat, those who come from "the grandmother" appreciate how spacious the cabin is compared to our old saddle. In the F1 you are more cloistered and have infinitely less vision, with the dome being much smaller and the front with hardly room for

In the Red Flag 2017/2, Eurofighter Typhoon fighters from Alas 11 and 14 from February 27 to March 10, 2017, participated in the Nellis air base (Nevada, USA).

Captain José Manuel Martínez Álvarez from Ala 11, after launching a GBU-16 - the explosion is seen in the upper right part of the photograph - during Red Flag 2017/2. [José Manuel Martínez Álvarez]

On the left is Major Álvaro José Navia-Osorio Torres accompanied by Captain Ignacio de los Pinos Díaz, who during a short time was the Ala 14 , since he has gone to Iberia (the Spanish flag carrier airline), being replaced by Captain Gregorio Serrano Arizaga. [S. Mafé]

the HUD. The feeling in the C.16 is to be higher and with more field of vision both front (with a HUD that looks like a widescreen compared to the F1) and lateral and rear thanks to its large dome.

The start-up is more automated and the engine parameters are controlled much less (since it is the aircraft itself that monitors the start-up and in case of any problem it would automatically abort it or even not let you start the start), however the workload is recovered at the time of initializing all the equipment (which are many) and perform all settings avionics, navigation and armament. The three huge screens presented by the C.16 are appreciated when it comes to having the best SA (awareness situation) during the combat, but they come to provide such amount of information that they can lead to saturation of the pilot if it is not managed correctly. It is at this moment where the before and after a Mirage pilot is marked, since during the first flights you have more than 90% of the information provided by the plane, accustomed to a single display and limitation of F1 equipment.

Once used to manage such a large amount of information, the C.16 flight becomes very simple thanks to the large number of automatisms that allow you to focus on combat management. The management of the communications is pleasantly more automatic and simple than in the F1, with a provision in the cabin and channeling of more practical and operative channels. Let's say that the C.16 is a "spaceship" which can be managed all from the same control panel, while "the grandmother" has all the controls spaced along the cabin.

At the moment of takeoff, you can see the incredible excess of power provided by the engines (it is such power that allows us to take off without afterburner and if we use it we must be agile and not be confused, since it is very easy to pass the speed limit of the train and even go from Mach 1 to take off), allowing to take off from almost any track and with minimal monitoring of the engines, unlike the F1 that you had to carefully monitor the parameters of your "only" engine during the takeoff race and was critical consideration of track distance and configuration type.

The navigation and ascent to the sector or zone of work is very simplified thanks to the multiple helps that the airplane provides us (aeronautical maps geo positioning, GPS, ...). This is another one of the moments in which you remember that black screen of "the grandmother"

with only 9 or 10 painted points and little else, which still seemed enough to go, "fight" and return from the area.

Once in the zone and after contacting all the participants of the mission (tactical controller and formations of both sides), the "fight's on" is sung and the combat begins. While the differences are remarkable at any stage of the flight with respect to the Mirage, it is here that you are really aware of the airplane (or rather, the weapons system) that you are driving. The great load capacity of armament in combination with an incredible radar and an avionics that fuses all the information shown on the screen, provide the pilot with an unbeatable SA for the combat, allowing a more effective and operative management of the armament that translates into a superiority overwhelming air (if the information is correctly managed). In addition, the C.16 has some engines and aerodynamics that allow it to maneuver at high speeds (supersonic) which further amplifies the effectiveness of the weaponry and tactical maneuvers.

If to all the above, we add the Link 16 capacity of the airplane, whose information merges perfectly with the aircraft, we can say that the SA we have is difficult to improve. Faced with this massive amount of information, the experience in an airplane like the F1 allows us to be prepared to continue fighting (even failing several of the advantageous systems that we have in the C.16), since this is how it is fought with the Mirage; with a precarious radar, limited maneuverability and avionics. And even in these conditions, the F1 pilots get to acquire a big SA (situational awareness) and face in an honorable way any opponent, being aware of their limitations.

The C.16 is an airplane that flies "fly by wire", that is to say, all the controls are directed by computers that obey to the commands of the

Various moments of the aerobatic display carried out by Captain Ignacio de los Pinos Díaz, former Ala 14 display pilot.

pilot, but limited within the envelope and capacities of the airplane. That is, no matter how much we want we can not pass the limitation of G's and even reached the loss point the plane automatically recovers the safe flight envelope. This is a crucial factor when it comes to combat, since unlike the F1 where it should be the pilot who controlled flying inside the flight envelope while managing the combat maneuvers (being much more demanding the flight), C.16 leaves the pilot with the sole task of managing the combat maneuver and can take the plane to the limit without exceeding it.

At the time of the RTB (return to the base), all the aids available (radar, MIDS, tactical

Captain José Manuel Martínez Álvarez, Ala 11 display pilot during a rehearsal. [José Figueredo López]

scenarios ...) allow you to take advantage of a more efficient time in flight, minimizing the deadlines of meeting, making everything more Fast and easy. It could be said that we could be confused with other traffics and join our training with the minimum use of radio, something unthinkable with F1."

The Eurofighter piloted by the captain José Manuel Martínez Álvarez, the Ala 11 display pilot during a rehearsal. [Jorge Portalés]

Eurofighter Typhoon of Ala 14 coming out of its hardened shelter on a training mission. Los Llanos and Gando are the only air bases that have HAS (Hardened Aircraft Shelters). [Jorge Portalés]

Captain Gregorio Serrano Arizaga, current pilot exhibitor of Ala 14. [G. Serrano]

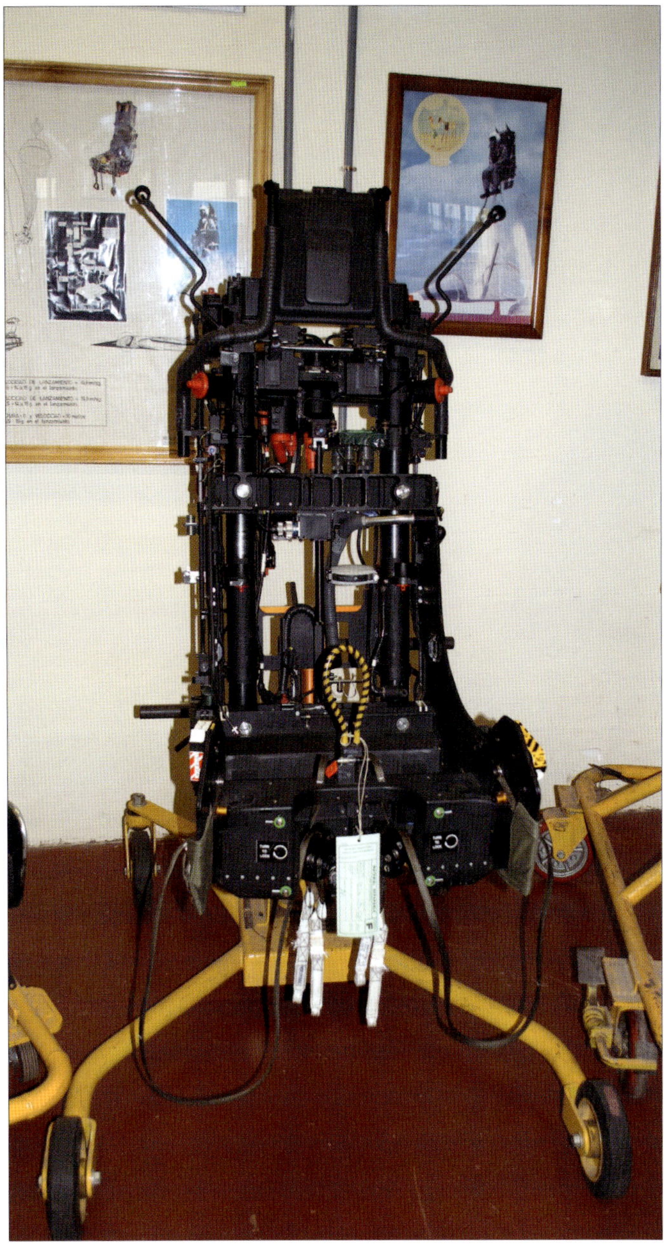

Training in Ala 14

To reach the maximum qualification (Package Lead) approximately 500 flight hours are needed and the previous qualifications have been achieved, which entails an approximate term of four years. The CR3 qualification could be obtained in less than two years, making the corresponding Basic Training Plans.

To make alarms it would be enough to be LCR and complete the in-processing and QRA upgrade, which is approximately 10 flights.

Currently, the annual schedule of flight hours for C.16 pilot are 140 plus 40 hours of simulator. However, a pilot can do more simulator hours, but never in exchange for flight hours.

Maintenance

The Maintenance Squadron of Ala 14 performs both Line Maintenance tasks as well as ML1 level of the C CE.16 Weapons System., also performs ML2 Maintenance tasks on a large part of the LRI/LRU of this Weapons System and the structural components of the aircraft. In addition,

The Albacete Air Depot (MAESAL) is a unit of the Air Force that, according to its structure, has an organic dependence on the General Air Command (MAGEN) and an operative unit of the Command of Logistic Support (MALOG). Its main mission is to support the weapons systems assigned to it at any moment by the Command at the level of the 3rd stage maintenance, carrying out fuselage checks, electronic equipment in this case of the Eurofighter, and also systems of survival, such as the Martin Baker Mk16A ejection seat. [Rafael Treviño Martínez]

Display pilots

The Spanish Air Force promotes its image, and very well by the way, with Patrulla Águila and the PAPEA (the parachute display team), but although less known, also really spectacular are the display pilots of the fighter units. The fighter planes are peculiar, they are very noisy, they have afterburners, and that makes them really showy. For the 2019 season, Ala 11 has Captain José Manuel Martínez, while Ala 14 had Captain Ignacio De Los Pinos Díaz, who in April 2019 was replaced by Captain Gregorio Serrano Arizaga of 142 Squadron, Captain Ignacio De Los Pinos went to Iberia. (All of them are very experienced pilots and they dominate the Eurofighter Typhoon perfectly.) Ignacio and then "Goyo" were handed over by Major Álvaro José Navia-Osorio Torres (see his story on previous pages). from takeoff to landing - about 16 minutes, and for better example we include this chart of the table developed by the pilot of Ala 14.

Maestranza Aérea de Albacete (MAESAL)

The Air Force Maintenance Depot of Albacete (MAESAL) is a unit of the Air Force that, according to its structure, has an organic dependency of the General Air Command (MAGEN) and an operational unit of the Logistic Support Command (MALOG).
Its main mission is to support the weapons systems assigned by the Command at the third step level and carry out major maintenance and repairs of the Eurofighter (C.16) deployed on Alas 11 and 14.
The Typhoon is a relatively new platform and none has yet to reach 2,000 flight hours, which is when it must undergo the third step revision; while and as support to the Maintenance Squadrons of both units, the second step revisions are made corresponding to the 500 / 1,000 flight hours.
In the area of engines, the Maestranza is responsible for the engineering, maintenance and supply of the EJ200 of the Eurofighter.
CLAEX (Logistics Center of Armament and Experimentation)
The CLAEX was created on March 15, 1991 as the heir of old units of the Air Force existing since 1946 for tasks related to the experimentation on land and in flight of aircraft, weapons and systems.
Maintaining the same hangar, designed by Eduardo Torroja in 1943, and considered as a singular structure due to its dimensions (182.88 meters long and 47.24 meters wide) and the fact that it has a single central column and a clearance 9 meters long, the CLAEX was created to be able to carry out the high-risk ground and flight tests carried out by its counterparts in allied countries.
Currently it has three Groups: Armament Group, Flight Test Group and Aeronautical Software Group and the Explosives Deactivation Center (CEOD) of the Air Force.
We are now focusing on the Aeronautical Software Group. Created in 1986 as a software support center to take on, among other tasks, the integration of armament and national software in the newcomers F-18, and having changed its initial denomination to those of Combat Informatics Group and Grupo de Computer science, since its inception has evolved to be able to design, validate, verify and currently maintain the on-board software of the F-5M F-18M and Typhoon airplanes supplied by the Air Force, as well as having a bank of tests for the detection of Eurofighter anomalies in coordination with the IWSSS (International Weapon System Support System). It has also developed operating software for Typhoon de la Tranche 1, for which the Austrian Air Force has been interested to update their own.

Simulators

The Weapons Instruction Center C.16 has two major areas: ASTA (Aircrew Synthetic Training Aids), recently renamed PSTS (Pilot Syntetic Training System) for the training of pilots, and GTA (Ground Trainign Aids for maintenance personnel.
The PSTS has two Full Mission Simulators (FMS) and a Cockpit Trainer / Interactive Pilot Station (CT / IPS) and are the flight simulators themselves, to which a Part Task Trainer (PTT) has been incorporated. The Wing 14 has a Part Task Trainer (PTT) and a Cockpit Trainer / Interactive Pilot Station (CT / IPS). The FMS has a dome with a 360º visual presentation, while the CT has a more limited visual. Both can operate in a network and have the necessary elements to generate scenarios and visual databases that allow to train complex missions with great realism.
The GTA has classrooms, simulators and computer aids for the training of maintenance and support personnel. It has three main components: Desk Top Trainer (DTT). Maintenance Simulator Trainer (MST) and the Crew Escape Safety System Trainer (CESST). The first two are multimedia systems, while the CESST is a full-scale replica of the cockpit with the ejection seat, which serves to train pilots and mechanics in the aircraft's exhaust system. Airbus and Indra, plus the German company KE, participate in the development, manufacture and update of these simulators.

The building of the ASTA (Aircrew Synthetic Training Aids), recently renamed PSTS (Pilot Syntetic Training System) for the training of pilots, and GTA (Ground Training Aids for maintenance personnel. [S. Mafé]

Consoles for the instructors in the PSTS, specifically for the FMS (Full Mission). [S. Mafé]

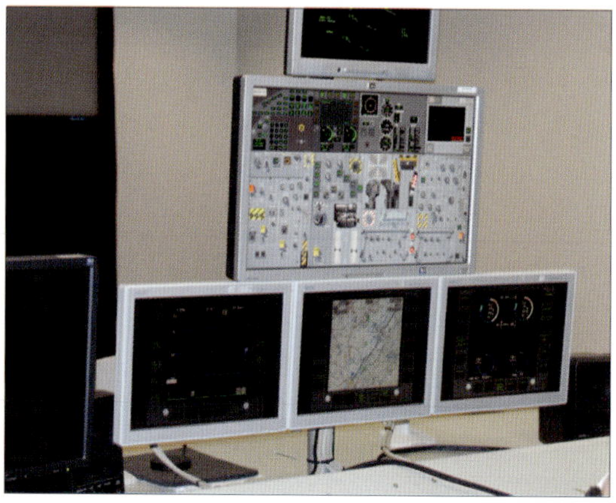

Interleaved with the simulator classes, the new Eurofighter pilots carry out their first "real" missions with the two-seater of the 113 Squadron. [S. Mafé]

General view of Cockpit Trainer (CT) of Ala 14. [Jorge Portalés]

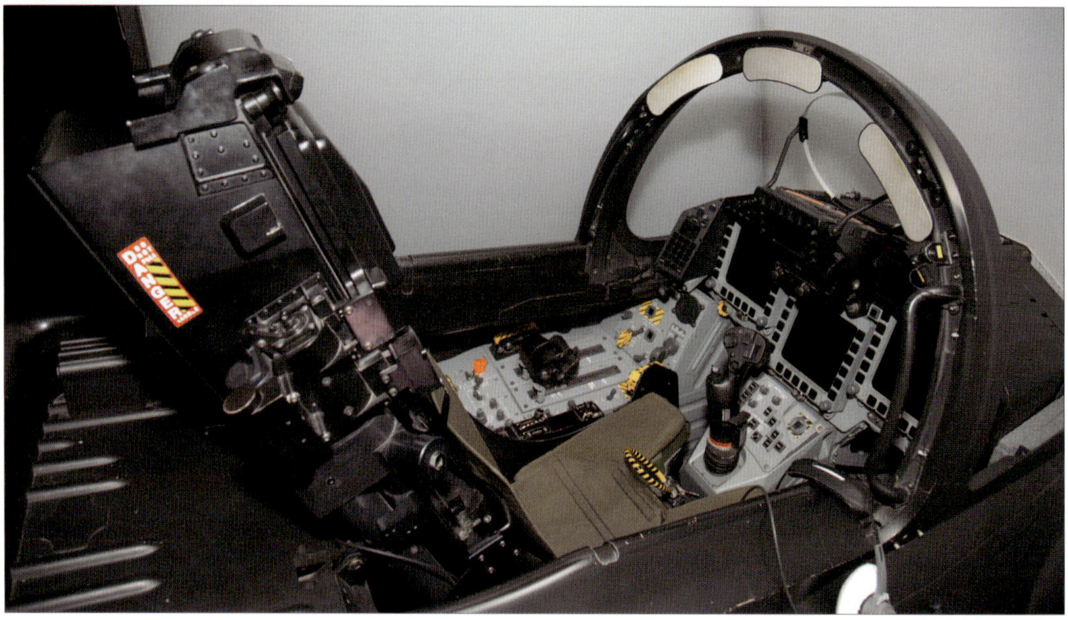

The FMS has a dome with a 360º visual presentation, while the CT has a more limited visual. Both can operate in a network and have the necessary elements to generate scenarios and visual databases that allow to train complex missions with great realism. [Jorge Portalés]

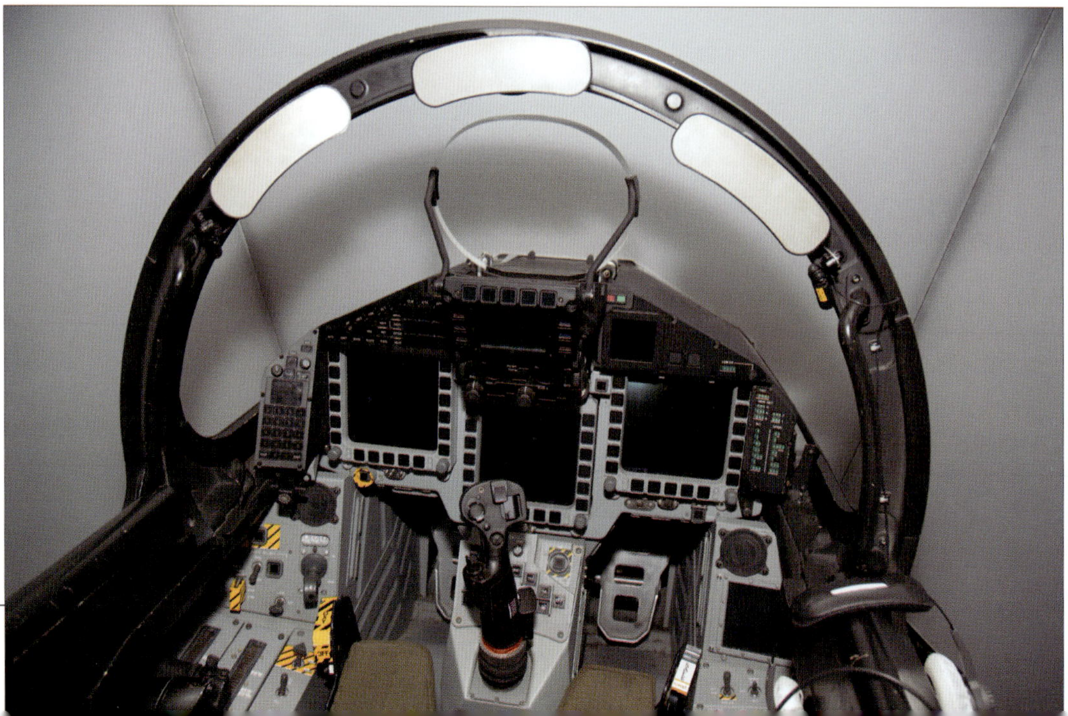

A pilot of the Luftwaffe in the Cockpit Trainer of Ala 11. [S. Mafé]

this Squadron also performs the maintenance of the assigned Ground Equipment.

As with most aircraft, the Maintenance Plan of the C.CE.16 is complex, performing pre- and post-flight inspections, periodic hourly inspections every 10, 25, 200, 400, 500 and 1,000 flight hours and their multiples, and inspections and maintenance actions, both by calendar, as shots or shots and releases or "on condition".

Capeval, dart and red flag

The first Capacity Assessment (CAPEVAL) from NATO to Grupo 11 of Ala 11. 1 was prepared thoroughly during 2016 for the evaluation of operational capacities (CAPEVAL ESPAF) of the 111 Squadron, which took place in October. As part of this preparation, and given the excellent relations between the Forces of both countries, the coincidence with the American tanker aircraft is exploited, also deployed at the Morón Air Base as part of the mission contingent SPMAGTF-CR-AF (US Marines Special-Purpose Marine Air-Ground Task Force Crisis Response-Africa), to perform refuelling missions in flight with their KC-130J Super Hercules.

These missions reveal very positive aspects: on the one hand, they reflect the agility in the processing of the corresponding procedures and authorizations; on the other hand, they demonstrate the interoperability between weapon systems of allied countries, as well as between components of different services of the Armed Forces, showing the progress of the Eurofighter in terms of the integration and certification of its operational capabilities.

But in reality the CAPEVAL are very demanding evaluations, which involve almost all aspects, in this case it was about measuring the operational capacity of the 111 Squadron, especially the loading and unloading of air-to-air weapons, one of the most demanding parts for the 111 Squadron was to overcome the permanent tension generated by the continuous "attacks" that it has to face during the more than two uninterrupted days that the CAPEVAL lasts. They had to face alleged attacks on the air base and dispersal zones of the Eurofighters by enemy snipers, harassment with mortars and rocket launchers, etc. also in "normal" environments, such as in NBQR environments, that is, contaminated by chemical or bacteriological weapons, so the personnel had to operate with the heavy and annoying protective equipment, ready so that when the alarm was sounded, in less than nine seconds , put on the masks and continue operating to continue maintaining and assembling the airplanes, and be able to fulfill the programmed departures. This evaluation simulates a zone of conflict quite realistically. Both the flight personnel, as mechanics, armourers, etc. They received the NATO certification, which indicates that the 111 Squadron can be deployed, practically to any place of conflict.

DART, the Typhoon sharpens its claws

During the week of November 5 to 9, 2018, the Dart exercise was held at the Morón de la Frontera Air Base (Seville); editions were also made in 2013, 2014 and 2015. The objective of this exercise is to perform real air-air shooting practices with the Air Force fighter aircraft (Eurofighter Typhoon and F/A-18A+ and EF-18M), as well as with the SHORAD air defense section

Grupo11 was prepared thoroughly during 2016 for the evaluation of operational capacities (CAPEVAL ESPAF) of the 111 Squadron, which took place in October. As part of this preparation, and given the excellent relations between the Forces of both countries, the coincidence with the American tanker aircraft is exploited, also deployed at the Morón Air Base as part of the mission contingent SPMAGTF-CR-AF (US Marines Special-Purpose Marine Air-Ground Task Force Crisis Response-Africa), to carry out air-to-air refuelling missions with their KC-130J Super Hercules. [Ala 11]

The CAPEVAL are very demanding evaluations, which involve almost all aspects, in this case it was about measuring the operational capacity of the 111 Squadron, especially the loading and unloading of air-to-air weapons, that is to say missiles AIM-120B AMRAAM and AIM-2000 IRIS-T, as well as munitions of the Mauser BK-27 27 mm cannon. One of the most demanding parts for the 111 Squadron was to overcome the permanent tension generated by the continuous "attacks" that it has to face during the more than two uninterrupted days that the CAPEVAL lasts. They had to face alleged attacks on the air base and dispersal zones of the Eurofighters by enemy snipers, harassment with mortars and rocket launchers, etc. also in "normal" environments, such as in NBQR environments, that is, contaminated by chemical or bacteriological weapons, so the personnel had to operate with the heavy and annoying protective equipment, ready so that when the alarm was sounded, in less than nine seconds , put on the masks and continue operating to continue maintaining and assembling the airplanes, and be able to fulfill the programmed departures. This evaluation simulates a zone of conflict quite realistically. Both the flight personnel, as mechanics, armourers, etc. They received the NATO certification, which indicates that the 111 Squadron can be deployed, practically to any place of conflict. [Ala 11]

Armourers with an AIM-2000 IRIS-T infrared guided AAM.

Also the Eurofighters have the AIM-9L Sidewinder. [Ala 11]

During the week of November 5 to 9, 2018 it was held at the Air Base from Morón de la Frontera (Seville) the Dardo (Dart) exercise; editions were also made in 2013, 2014 and 2015. The objective of this exercise is to perform real air-air shooting practices with the Air Force fighter aircraft (Eurofighter Typhoon and F/A-18A+ and EF-18M), as well as with the SHORAD air defense section of short-range anti-aircraft missiles belonging to the Air Deployment Support Squadron (EADA), for the towing of targets there was a Dassault Falcon 20 from the French company AVdef, under whose left plane it carried a target for infrared missiles and another for radar missiles. [Wing 11]

During this shooting campaign, eight IRIS-T missiles, three AIM-7 Sparrow missiles and two Aspide missiles were launched. The latter were launched from the ground at the Medano del Loro shooting range in Huelva by the EADA. Alas 11, 12, 14, 15 and 46 participated in this campaign. They had the support of the Mobile Air Control Group (GRUMOCA) and the Logistics Center of Support and Experimentation (CLAEX). In addition, Wing 48 gave SAR coverage to the exercise. The Combat Air Command (MACOM) was responsible for the planning and execution of the campaign. The launches took place in limited areas of the Gulf of Cádiz, with the collaboration of the company SCR, which is in charge of providing the targets to shoot down. These are aircraft piloted from the ground (drones) capable of flying in formation and maneuvering as if they were in a real tactical scenario, in addition to the targets towed by the Falcon. This training system allows fighter pilots to train not only in missile firing, but also in air-to-air combat tactics. In DART 2013, 2014 and 2015 it was in the last ones that Group 11 used the short-range and infrared guided missiles AIM-9L Sidewinder. [Wing 11]

of short-range anti-aircraft missiles belonging to the Air Deployment Support Squadron (EADA).

During this shooting campaign, eight IRIS-T missiles, three AIM-7 Sparrow missiles and two Aspide missiles were launched. The latter were launched from the ground at the Medano del Loro shooting range in Huelva by the EADA.

Alas 11, 12, 14, 15 and 46 participated in this campaign. They had the support of the Mobile Air Control Group (GRUMOCA) and the Logistics Center of Support and Experimentation (CLAEX). In addition, Ala 48 Super Puma helicopters gave SAR coverage to the exercise. The Combat Air Command (MACOM) was responsible for the planning and execution of the campaign.

The launches took place in limited areas of the Gulf of Cádiz, with the collaboration of the company SCR, which is in charge of providing the targets to shoot down. These are aircraft piloted from the ground capable of flying in formation and maneuvering as if they were in a real tactical scenario.

This training system allows fighter pilots to train not only in missile firing, but also in air-to-air combat tactics.

Spanish Typhoon Eurofighters in Red Flag

The Air Force took stock of the Red Flag in which Eurofighter Typhoon fighters participated from February 27 to March 10, 2017 at Nellis Air Base (Nevada, USA). In these maneuvers eight Spanish fighters took part, belonging to Ala 11 (Morón Air Base, Seville) and Ala 14 (Albacete Air Base), and two KC-130H Hercules (Ala 31, Zaragoza air base) that formed a Expeditionary Air Group. A total of 230 Spanish military were also supported by two Italian KC-767 tankers.

During this edition, close to 165 aircraft belonging to the participating countries were gathered: the United States, the Netherlands, Singapore and Spain; with a variety of roles.

Here are some conclusions analyzed by the Air Force and released in a statement:

1. The objective: was to operate for the first time with the Eurofighters more than 5,000 nau-

The Air Combat Command (MACOM) led the participation in this second edition of the year of the Red Flag exercise. The Spanish AF is considered the most complex and demanding exercise in air warfare among those organized worldwide. The most operational air forces participate in it, under the direction of the United States Air Force (USAF). It takes place at the base of Nellis (Nevada), near the city of Las Vegas. I fly during its jump from the Atlantic and will stop at the Lajes air base, in the Azores Islands (Portugal), and at the air base of the USAF in Dover, on the east coast of the United States. Later they will make the last jump to Nellis. A P-3 Orion from Group 22 and a CN-235 from VIGMA maritime surveillance from the 48th Wing complete the device, taking charge of SAR support for the ocean crossing. On board, a team of parachutist rescuers from the Parachutist Sapper Squadron, who in the event of one of the planes falling into the sea, would be in charge of the pilot's rescue. Everything must be in place when it comes to flight safety. To participate in the Red Flag exercise, the Air Force has established an Expeditionary Air Group. The bulk of the group is made up of pilots, mechanics, and gunsmiths from the 14th and 11th Wing, who provide the Eurofighter aircraft. In addition to other units that contribute by providing essential capacities for grouping. Thus, the Air Combat Command (MACOM) contributes the command post personnel, specialized in the direction of the group, including the chief, who during the exercise, will have the same responsibilities as the force chiefs in real operations abroad. The Weapons and Experimentation Logistics Center (CLAEX) contributes with specialized personnel in the assembly of the real weapons that will be used during the exercise. The Madrid Air Deployment Support Medical Unit (UMAAD Madrid) provides the group's health personnel. (Description for photos on pages 95 and 96) [Photos: EdA]

tical miles (nm) from Spain, in addition to the integration in an international coalition, in which capabilities in combined offensive and defensive air operations could be tested, within very demanding complex scenarios, close to reality and high threat density.

2. Two sides: the participating forces were divided into two camps, the "Blue", simulating an International coalition in which Spanish aircraft were integrated along with most of the aerial resources of the US Air Force (USAF), such as aircraft F-15, F-18, KC-135, C-130 Hercules, etc., in addition to the Dutch F-16s and the CH-47 helicopters from Singapore.

On the other hand, opposition forces, the "Red" side, with F-16 of the 64th Agressor Squadron of the USAF simulating flight profiles of MiG-29 and Su-30 and electronic warfare aircraft. there were only aerial threats, also participated up to 26 real surface-air systems and simulated emitters, in addition to smoke rockets systems to simulate surface-to-air missile launches, "according to the statement of the Air Force.

3. Area of the exercises: it covered an area of about 150 nautical miles for 110 nautical miles and in it several scenarios based on defensive air missions were simulated in order to maintain the

defense of sensitive points; scenarios oriented to offensive air missions against the adversary's air defense system; scenarios in which the search and location of targets in motion is considered; and, finally, scenarios in which the rescue of a downed pilot with HH-60 helicopter protection and escort fighters, support and air defense is simulated.

4. The Spanish Eurofighters made 104% of departures: during the development of the exercise, the Eurofighters made 157 departures, not counting the deployment and withdrawal flights, or, what is the same, 104% of the scheduled missions. On the other hand, the Hercules planes made 12 sorties, both in air refueling missions and tactical air transport, achieving 100% of the scheduled missions.

5. Conclusion: In short, the participation of the Air Force, for the second time in a row, in the last eight years, has been a success not only from the point of view of the operation and maintenance of aircraft, in which It has achieved more than 100% of the scheduled departures for both weapons systems, but also has been able to verify the high degree of preparedness of our crews and the specialist mechanical and armored personnel when facing the different incidents, as well such as the handling and assembly of the air-ground weapon.

A mission in the Red Flag

Captain Joaquin Ducay de la Riva, pilot of 111 Squadron, tells us about the development of a mission during Red Flag:

Buick 51 flight, pushing. "It is already" -I thought- "to get them". With this call we announced that we were crossing the border and entering enemy territory under cover of the night. We were a pair of Eurofighters of Ala 11, armed with two live GBU-16s each, two AIM-120 AMRAAM missiles and two oIRIS-T (all simulated). But we were not alone. There were more than 70 combat and support aircraft perfectly coordinated to carry out the mission.

Our formation had ordered an attack on communication nodes that would allow us to degrade the integrity of the early warning and enemy air defense, but we were not the first to enter the combat zone. When we were doing the push, most of the "package" friend was already attacking the possible threats.

In flight, and especially when a combat begins, you seldom have half a second free to think of something alien to what is immediately priority: the mission. But once in a while you have small instants, always fleeting, in which a tumult of sensations pass through your head. This was one of them.

Being aware that, despite being already flying over enemy territory, the war was still far away (understood by just a minute and a half) my mind derived a fraction of his attention for half a second to "stop" to think: " here we are".

"Here we are" summarized perfectly in one sentence everything that I felt: a complete satisfaction for being able to be enjoying that experience, those landscapes, those sensations and that adrenaline; gratitude for being able to be there flying together with my colleagues and with other countries; a deep sense of accomplishment.

In the initial stretch of the route, our goal was to defend ourselves against any threat that might arise. We were waiting for the alert and radar of the enemy SAM, pending with our radar to attack and shoot down any enemy air trace that slipped from the first wave of pure air-air fighters, and looking at the ground looking for "flashes" of possible launches of said SAM.

We were more than illuminated by the SAM's early warning and search radars, but still out of reach, so the biggest concern was to "sanitize" the aerial space by making sure there were no "smart-ass" enemy fighters stuck to the ground. behind a mountain waiting to ambush us.

On this flight we did not find any, but on the way to the target, a couple of F-16 aggressors (enemies) had sneaked in and crossed the defensive barrier of the air-to-air fighters. They were not yet a threat factor for us, but for other formations that, probably given their technical capabilities, were not fully aware that they were being threatened.

But our plane did see them. I saw our radar, our interrogator declared them enemies and the picture that AWACS was passing through the MIDS. Once with the certainty of being in compliance with the ROE and with the positive declaration of the GCI, my Buick 51 training, we launched a simulated AMRAAM to each hostile contact while we continued with our route.

Soon, the missiles were reaching their targets with high probability of success, and the attackers withdrew as "dead".

When the warnings started in the alert that they were firing SAM against us, we reacted instinctively according to our SOP (standard operating procedures) and maneuvered according to the threat, while throwing chaff and flares (radar and infrared lures).

The night was illuminated with flashes in our tails. While we were maneuvering, I could see that the whole sky was illuminated by flares in different places and at different heights. None of the fighters in the area had the lights on, so all the lights that shone from a flash and went off in the area were those of other friendly planes defending themselves.

It was time to attack. As a lesson learned from previous flights we realized that the aggressors were tremendously astute at attacking unnoticed just as the fighters are launching their air-ground weaponry (and that it is in turn when they are most vulnerable). For this reason, and given that in this mission we had a very wide

The current TaktLwG 74), based in Neuburg, received its first aircraft on July 25, 2006. The unit is part of the Luftwafe Reaction Force, and is assigned to the NATO Response Force. Here we see the 20 + 28 during a TLP landing at Los Llanos. [Juan José Fernández]

window / attack range, we decided that we would adapt some tactics that would allow us to cover each other without the need of support from other planes. It was the closest thing to a pair of infantry or a pair of attack helicopters: one of the fighters was orbiting perpendicularly to the axis of threat over his partner while it attacked the targets on the ground covering it in case any threat entered, and once the first one beat its targets, the roles were reversed.

And so it was done, and so we killed another two enemy fighters who tried to surprise us, what a sensation it is to be firing a missile while the sky is full of flares and the ground lights up with the flashes of bombs of your formation exploding on their targets! . A combination of adrenaline, satisfaction, and doubt when considering if in case of being a real mission, in a real theater of operations, there would be place in my head for the "fear".

Miller time: last target down. We are returning to Nellis after a successful mission.

RED FLAG 2020-2

RED FLAG is a contested combat training exercise involving the air forces of the United States and its allies. It is coordinated at Nellis Air Force Base, Nevada, and conducted on the vast bombing and gunnery ranges of the Nevada Test and Training Range (NTTR). It is one of a series of advanced training programs administered by the United States Air Force Warfare Center and Nellis Air Force Base.

RED FLAG was established in 1975 as the brain child of Lt. Col. Richard "Moody" Suter and one of the initiatives directed by General Robert J. Dixon, then commander of Tactical Air Command, to better prepare our forces for combat. Lessons from Vietnam showed that if a pilot survived his first 10 combat missions, his probability of survival for remaining missions increased substantially. Red Flag was designed to expose each "Blue 4" pilot to his first 10 "combat missions" here at Nellis, allowing him to be more confident and effective in actual combat. This same principle continues to guide Red Flag today, with the goal of preparing Air Force, Joint, and Coalition pilots, aircrew and operators to fight against a peer-level adversary in any combat environment.

Tasked to plan and control this training, the 414th Combat Training Squadron's mission is to maximize the combat readiness, capability and survivability of participating units by providing realistic, multi-domain training in a combined air, ground, space and electronic threat environment while providing opportunity for a free exchange of ideas between forces.

Aircraft and personnel deploy to Nellis for RED FLAG under the Air Expeditionary Force concept and make up the exercise's "Blue" forces. By working together, these Blue forces are able to utilize their diverse capabilities to execute specific missions, such as air interdiction, combat search and rescue, close air support, dynamic targeting and defensive counter air. These forces use various tactics to attack NTTR targets such as mock airfields, vehicle convoys, tanks, parked aircraft, bunkered defensive positions and missile sites. These targets are defended by a variety of simulated "Red" force ground and air threats to give participant aircrews the most realistic combat training possible.

The Red force threats are aligned under the 57th Adversary Tactics Group, which controls seven squadrons of USAF Aggressors, including fighter, space, information operations and air defense units. The Aggressors are specially trained

An Ala 11 Typhoon, landing at Gando air base, after a defensive counter air mission during Ocean Sky 21.

to replicate the tactics and techniques of potential adversaries and provide a scalable threat presentation to Blue forces which aids in achieving the desired learning outcomes for each mission.

A typical RED FLAG exercise involves a variety of attack, fighter and bomber aircraft (F-15E, F-35, F-16, F/A-18, A-10C, B-1B, B-2A, B-52H, FGR4, MQ-9, etc.), reconnaissance aircraft (MQ-4B, RC-135, U-2S), electronic warfare aircraft (EC-130H, EA-18G and F-16CM), air superiority aircraft (F-22A, F-15C, etc), airlift support (C-130, C-17A), Search and Rescue aircraft (HH-60G, HC-130J, CH-47), aerial refueling aircraft (KC-130, KC-135R, KC-10A, etc), multi-domain Command and Control platforms (E-3, E-8C, E-2C, E-7, R1, etc) as well as ground based Command and Control, Space, and Cyber Forces.

Four U.S. military services, their Guard/Reserve components and the air forces of other countries participate in each RED FLAG exercise. Since 1975, 29 countries have joined the U.S. in these exercises and several other countries have participated as observers. RED FLAG has provided training for more than 506,000 military personnel, including more than 157,000 aircrew members flying more than 411,000 sorties and logging more than 757,000 hours of flying time.

Eight Spanish Typhoons went Nellis Air Force Base For Red Flag 20-2

Ten Spanish Air Force Eurofighter Typhoons, pooled from ALA11 and 14, split in two cells and supported by 2x RAF A330 Voyager tankers deplyoed late in Febebruary 2020 to Nellis AFB where they took part in RF 20-2. The Eurocanard aircraft along with their SAR support party made of a P3M P.3M-08/22-31 and a CN235 T.19B-12/D.4-01 along with a KC-130H TK.10-11/31-53 (that carried the support team), made a stopover in Lajes, Azores, on Feb. 29, 2020, before continuing their trip across the Pond via Dover AFB on Mar. 1.

Only eight aircraft eventually deployed as two Typhoons acted as spares.

Noteworthy one the Eurofighters (C.16-73 /14-31) is the Typhoon that was prepared for the NATO Tiger Meet 2018 and sports its distinctive specail "Tiger tail".

First cell:

- AME1401 EF2000A C.16-45/14-10 ALA14,
- AME1402 EF2000A C.16-62 10047 /14-21 ALA14,
- AME1403 EF2000A C.16-74 10202 /14-32 ALA14,
- AME1404 EF2000A C.16-73 /14-31 ALA14,
- AME1405 EF2000T CE.16-12 10000 /14-71 ALA14,
- RRR9211 A332 ZZ338.

Second cell:

- AME1406 EF2000T CE.16-14 10015 /11-14 ALA11,
- AME1407 EF2000A C.16-43 /11-43 ALA11,

Close-up of an Ala 14 two-seater.

- AME1408 EF2000A C.16-52 11052 /11-52 ALA11,
- AME1409 EF2000A C.16-35 /11-35 ALA11,
- AME1410 EF2000A C.16-64 10053 /14-22 ALA14,
- RRR9212 A332 ZZ335.

Support a/c:

- AME3130 KC130H TK.10-11/31-53,
- AME4810 CN235 T.19B-12 / D.4-01,
- AME2206 P-3M P.3M-08/22-31.

Interestingly, Red Flag 2020-1 was sort-of "European Red Flag" considered that along with the Spanish team, it was attended by Italian F-35A and F-2000 Typhoons, and by the German Eurofighters.

Ocean Sky 21

MACOM (ESP AF Air Combat Command), as the Command in charge of the preparation of ESP AF Air Combat units, Combat Support units, and of the Air Surveillance and Control System, will carry out an advanced Air-to-Air training exercise in the airspace south of the Canary Islands which will comprise large-scale DCA, OCA and other Counter-Air supporting missions.

The authority scheduling the exercise is the ESP AF Chief of Staff (JEMA – OSE), the authority conducting the exercise is MACOM Commander (GJMACOM – OCE), and the authority directing the exercise is MACOM Chief of Staff (GJEMMACOM – ODE/EXDIR). The Chief of MACOM Training and Evaluation Branch will act as Deputy Exercise Director (Chief A7 – DEPEXDIR).

Apart from its permanent mission of defending the Spanish sovereign airspace, the ESP AF must maintain its units adequately trained and ready to be transferred to the operational structure of the ESP Armed Forces whenever they are activated to participate in real operations.

Ocean Sky 21 strategic conditions

The possible integration of ESP AF Combat units, Combat Support units, Deployment Support units and Command and Control units in real operations of a joint/combined nature, requires those units to be appropriately trained and evaluated in the broad spectrum of capabilities they possess. In this respect, the evolution of potential threats and the various contingencies they would have to face demands their training to be increasingly specialized, realistic, and comprising the various types of missions associated to their capabilities. More particularly, the evolution of Air-to-Air tactics, techniques and procedures and the development of new capabilities associated with advances in long-range Air-to-Air missiles, requires very specific airspace and complex mission design in order to obtain high quality training.

Ocean Sky 21 objectives

Exercise OS21 has the following general objectives:

- Train and evaluate ESP AF Air units in the Counter-Air core air power role, by planning and executing the following types of operations alongside allied air forces´ units:

- Defensive Counter, Air (DCA):

Combat Air Patrol (Area Defence, Point Defence and HVAA Protection).

- Offensive Counter, Air (OCA):

Fighter Sweep (COMAO, HVAA Attack). Escort (Close Escort and Detached Escort).

- Train and evaluate ESP AF Air units in the Air Mobility core air power role, by planning and executing the following types of operations alongside allied air forces´ units in the framework of the EART:

- Air-to-Air Refueling (AAR):

Theater Support.

- Train and evaluate the ESP AF Air Surveillance and Control System (ASACS) by planning and executing support to OCA and DCA missions in the form of tactical assistance and control.

- Train the ESP AF Aerospace Operations Center on the tasks of planning, tasking, supervising, assessing and reporting on air operations of all allocated assets in accordance with higher level directives and guidance, and lower level reports.

- Train MACOM Staff personnel in the planning, direction, control and evaluation process of an air exercise.

- Promote interoperability, trust, and mutual understanding among national and foreign participants „

Typhoon users

The Eurofighter Typhoon is the only modern fighter aircraft that has different assembly lines (the F-35 is only produced internationally under limited licenses, in Italy and Japan). Each partner assembles its own aircraft, although it builds the same parts of all the aircraft that are produced.

Germany

The German plans provided for the purchase of 180 Eurofighter, including single-seater EF2000 and two-seater EF2000T (the name Typhoon is not used).

They should have delivered 44 planes from Tranche 1 and 68 from each of Tranches 2 and 3, equipping five wings. Eleven Tranche 1 were diverted to Austria and replaced by additional Tranche 2.

In October 2011 the German Ministry of Defense issued a major restructuring of the program, canceling the last batch of 37 Tranche 3B. Thus the production was limited to 143 aircraft: 33 Tranche 1, 79 Tranche 2 and 31 Tranche 3A.

The Eurofighter equips three wings, each with 31 aircraft; a smaller one with 20 and an operational training unit with 24. All wings of hunting and bombing hunts (Jagdgeschwader and Jadgdbombersgeschwader: JG - JBG) changed their denomination on October 1, 2013 as Taktisches Luftwaffengeschwader / Tactical Wings of the Air Force , abbreviated TaktLwG.

The first production example for the Luftwaffe made its initial flight on February 13, 2003, before being transferred to the technical school of Kaufbeuren where it was used as a training element for mechanics and other specialties, to later be updated to the standard Block 5 and delivered to a unit three years later.

The first unit of the Luftwaffe was the Jagdgeschwader 73 (JG 73) "Steinhoff" based on Laage, receiving the first three Eurofighter arrived on April 26, 2004. The unit is currently known as TaktLwG 73 "Steinhoff".

The second wing to be converted, JG 74 (TaktLwG 74), based in Neuburg, received its first aircraft on July 25, 2006. The unit is part of the Luftwafe Reaction Force, and is assigned to the Air Force Response Force. NATO

The first wing of Tornado to re-equip with the Eurofighter, JBG 31 (TaktLwG 31) "Boelkle" based in Nörvenich, received its first two aircraft on December 16, 2009, its pilots began an intense preparation in air-ground tactics, using the Tornado tactics manual, before receiving the P1E update, which in turn involved the integration of the Litening III designator pod and the Raytheon GBU-48 Enhanced Paveway II pump with 454 kg and dual guidance, laser / GPS.

The fourth unit was JG 71 "Richthofen" (TaktLwG 71) in Wittmund, although initially it only operates a squadron (staffel) with 20 aircraft.

The German Eurofighters are armed with the AIM-120B AMRAAM missile and IRIS-T for air-to-air, although the first is in the process of being replaced by the Meteor. For the air-ground role it has the GBU-48, some of them with the Trojan penetrating head (TIP). The Luftwaffe hopes to integrate the RecceLite reconnaissance pod, the Taurus cruise missile and new weapons, such as the HOSBO (German acronym for a high-performance penetrating bomb), the Small Diameter Bomb and the Pilum light missile.

Two German Eurofighter jets collide in training, one pilot dead

Two Eurofighter EF-2000s of the Luftwaffe, the German Air Force, collided during a training mission. While both pilots managed to eject, one of them was found dead.

The first unit of the Luftwaffe was the Jagdgeschwader 73 (JG 73) "Steinhoff" based on Laage, receiving the first three Eurofighter arrived on April 26, 2004. The unit is currently known as TaktLwG 73 "Steinhoff "It was her honor, among the four partners of the program, to celebrate the 500,000 flight hours of the European fighter plane. [Eurofighter]

The two aircraft "were on an Air Combat Mission with a third Eurofighter. The pilot of the third Eurofighter observed the collision and said he saw two parachutes land," said the Luftwaffe on Twitter, adding in a press release that the fighter jets were not armed. The three EF-2000s involved belonged to the Taktisches Luftwaffengeschwader (Tactical Air Force Wing) 73 "Steinhoff" based at Laage Airport near Rostock, northeastern Germany.

The two crash sites were found ten kilometers apart. One of the pilots was found after he landed in a tree, and was taken to a hospital. As for the second one, he was not immediately located. The Luftwaffe announced later that he did not survive to the ejection.

Debris was scattered over a vast area and the local population has been asked not to approach it. Der Spiegelreported that two firefighters were slightly injured after inhaling toxic fumes. Operations to secure the crash sites and recover debris continued late into the night and could last for a whole week. The flight recorders were recovered on June 25, 2019.

German Defense Minister Ursula von der Leyen expressed her sympathy to the pilot's relatives and thanked the forces and people for their help "at this difficult hour," before announcing the opening of an investigation. The other fighter jets of the Tactical Air Force Wing 73 have been grounded.

It is the second time in recent years that an EF-2000 of the Luftwaffe is involved in a deadly crash. In June 2014, one of the fighter jets belonging to Tactical Air Force Wing 31 based in Nörvenich Air Base collided with a Learjet that was acting as a target during an interception exercise. While the EF-2000 managed to land safely, the Learjet crashed, killing its two occupants.

Saudi Arabia

After a series of negotiations between the Saudi government and the United Kingdom in 2005, the "Salam Project" was signed in August 2007, covering the purchase of 72 Typhoon for Al Quwwat al Jawwiiya as Saúdiya (Royal Saudi Air Force - RFAS), together with training, support and technology transfer agreements.

The agreement between the two governments with BAE Systems acting as prime contractor, included an assembly line in Saudi Arabia, although the first 24 aircraft were diverted from orders of Tranche 2 of the RAF.

The first Saudi aircraft, made its initial flight on October 20, 2008, and was officially delivered to the RFAS on June 11, 2009. The first two went into service with the 3 Squadron at the Taif air base twelve days later.

The first eight Saudi Typhoons wore the emblem of 10 Squadron, leading many to assume that the unit was formed to act as an operational conversion unit. Eventually the 3 Squadron was formed before being appointed as OCU, while also maintaining an operational role.

The Unit started to carry out alarms (QRA) in mid-2011, before starting an intensive training in air-ground operations in December 2011, which included the Paveway II and Enhanced Paveway II bombs and the Damocles designator pod -of French origin- being the only Typhoon operator that uses it (although Kuwait and Qatar will also use it). The RFAS was the first to use the

The German Eurofighters are armed with the AIM-120B AMRAAM missile and IRIS-T for air-to-air, although the first one is in the process of being replaced by the Meteor. For the air-ground role it has the GBU-48, some of them with the Trojan penetrating head (TIP). The Luftwaffe hopes to integrate the RecceLite reconnaissance pod, the Taurus cruise missile and new weapons, such as the HOSBO (German acronym for a high-performance penetrating bomb), the Small Diameter Bomb and the Pilum light missile. [Eurofighter]

Tranche 2 in air-ground, other operators waited for the P1EA update.

Following the delivery of the 24 Eurofighters manufactured in Warton on September 22, 2011, production should have been moved to new facilities at the air base at King Abdul Aziz in Dhahran. But although the construction of the technical zone and BAE Systems had begun to train the Saudis in the assembly plant in Warton, the industrial program did not materialize.

It was concluded that local participation in the support throughout the life of the aircraft would have more benefits than the final assembly, so at the beginning of 2012 a modification was

The Saudi Typhoons operate as "swing-role" fighters, that is they can change configuration in mid-flight, being armed with AMRAAM missiles (Meteor is becoming available) and IIRS-T , as well as the Storm Shadow, Paveway IV and Brimstone. The photographs, of course, are not taken in Saudi Arabia, but in an air festival held in Austria. [Eurofighter]

signed in the 72 aircraft of the "Salam Project", continuing the manufacture of the remaining appliances in the United Kingdom.

The first aircraft of this second batch made its initial flight from Warton on November 30, 2012, and deliveries were resumed in June 2013. The arrival of the new aircraft allowed the activation of the 10 Squadron (the second unit of Typhoon) in Taif.

As part of the negotiations, the last 24 planes are from Tranche 3A, carrying out its inaugural flight on March 13, 2015, being delivered on June 5. Some of the last ones delivered carry the emblem of the 80 Squadron, while also and later the 15 Squadron was activated.

It is believed that there are negotiations for additional orders. The Saudi Typhoons operate as "swing-role" fighters, ie they can change configura-

tion in mid-flight, being armed with missiles AMRAAM (soon to have Meteor) and IIRS-T, as well as the Storm Shadow, Paveway IV and Brimstone.

Austria

It was the first export customer of the Eurofighter (it did not adopt the name Typhoon), agreeing to purchase 18 Tranche 3 aircraft on July 1, 2003, to eventually confirm the order for 15 single-seater Tranche 1 Block 5 for the Osterreichische Luftstreitkrafte (Air Force Austrian). They were manufactured using production slots from the four partner countries (being replaced by Tranche 2 aircraft for Germany, Spain, Italy and the United Kingdom, 11 came from Germany, two from the United Kingdom, and one from each of Spain and Italy. they entered service on July 12, 2007 with the Air Surveillance Wing (Überwachungsgeschwader), based Weltweg / Steiermark, while the latter was delivered in Manching on September 24, 2009. Pilots and ground personnel received their training with the then JG 73 of Laage.

These aircraft replaced 12 F-5E Tiger II rented to the Swiss Air Force, which in turn had replaced the Saab J35 Draken vtereans in 2004-2005. Armed only with the short-range air-to-air missile IRIS-T, the surveillance work on Austrian airspace began on July 1, 2008.

The Tranche 1 of the Alpine country have the Service Release Proposal 4.3 software, new radios, GPS and IFF. Although a judicial inquiry into the

The first of the 15 Austrian Eurofighters entered service on July 12, 2007 with the Air Surveillance Wing (Überwachungsgeschwader), based Weltweg / Steiermark, while the latter was delivered in Manching on 24 September 2009. Pilots and ground crew received their training with the then JG 73 of Laage. [Eurofighter]

manner in which the aircraft were purchased from Airbus is under way, and some informal statements claim that the Eurofighters would be withdrawn from service after 2020, the fact is that they will remain in service for many more years and it is possible that acquire the updates that have been applied, apply and apply to the Spanish Tranche 1.

Italy

The Aeronautica Militare Italiana (AMI) had planned to receive 121 Eurofighter F-2000A (native denomination) and 15 TF-2000A two-seaters. According to the original plan 29 planes would be from Tranche 1, plus 46 from each of Tranches 2 and 3. After the cuts of all partners of the program Italy is with 29 Tranche 1, 47 Tranche 2 and 21 Tranche 3A .

It was planned to equate six stormi (wings) with six gruppi (squadrons), ie 4th Stromo at Grossseto, 36th Stormo at Gioia del Colle and 37th Stormo at Trapani-Bergi, but the aforementioned cuts forced a revised plan to equip two squadrons the wings of Grosseto and Giogia, while that of Trapani was left with only one.

The first unit of the AMI to be converted was the 4th Stormo in Grosseto, which received its first TF-2000A on March 18, 2004, forming two squadrons: 9th Gruppo (operative) and 10º Gruppo (operational conversion). On December 10, 2015, the 4th Stormo began to perform

The first unit of the AMI to become the Eruofighter was the 4th Stormo in Grosseto, which received its first TF-2000A on March 18, 2004, forming two squadrons : 9th Gruppo (operative) and 10th Gruppo (operative conversion). On December 10, 2015, the 4th Stormo began to perform the alarm service (QRA), being the first of the four partners to carry it out. On July 1, 2007 to the 37th Stormo, his arrival allowed the activation of the 12th Gruppo and later of his second squadron the 10th Gruppo "Picca". On May 23, 2012, the 18th Gruppo "Brandy", the only Eurofighter squadron of the 37th Stromo, concluded its conversion, its first plane having arrived in Trapani four months earlier. Like the Air Force, the AMI could acquire more Eurofighter to compensate the reduction in the purchase of F-35A Lightning II, which will receive 75 of this variant. (Description for photos on pages 105 and 106) [S. Mafé, C. Schrik, Eurofighter]

the alarm service (QRA), being the first of the four partners to carry it out. On July 1, 2007 to the 37th Stormo, his arrival allowed the activation of the 12th Gruppo and later of his second squadron the 10th Gruppo "Picca". On May 23, 2012, the 18th Gruppo "Brandy", the only Eurofighter squadron of the 37th Stromo, concluded its conversion, its first plane having arrived in Trapani four months earlier. Like the Air Force, the AMI could acquire more Eurofighter to compensate the reduction in the purchase of F-35A Lightning II, which will receive 75 of this variant.

Oman

In December 2015, BAE Systems announced an order from the Sultanate of Oman for 12 Typhoon de la Tranche 3A (nine single-seaters and three two-seaters). The first two two - both tandem - flew for the first time from Warton on November 25, 2017, beginning in early 2018 deliveries to Silah al-Jaww Sultany 'Uman (Royal Air Force of Oman) where he has equipped the 8 Squadron in Thumrait, which until 2014 operated the Jaguar.

UK

The original requirement of the United Kingdom consisted of 202 Eurofighter (known since 2002 as Typhoon) - 55 of Tranche 1, 88 Tranche 2 and 89 of Tranche 3.

It is expected with these 232 aircraft to equip seven first-line RAF squadrons, the first two at RAF Coningsby, Lincolnshire, with the ADX (all-weather air defense) mission initially assigned from 2005.

They were followed by three FBC squadrons (hunting-bombing), two in RAF Leeming, North Yorkshire between 2006 and 2007 and another in RAF Leuchar Fife, in 2008.

Finally the polyvalent squadrons would be activated in RAF Leuchars (2009-2010). All units were scheduled to make the transition to "swing-role" operations when the seventh squadron formed.

These plans have changed and in total 160 aircraft have been purchased for the RAF. 53 of Tranche 1 (two were diverted to Austria), 67 of Tranche 2 (including two additional as compensation for those delivered to Austria, plus an Instrumented Series Production Aircraft (ISPA),

The first RAF aircraft, license plate ZJ803, was delivered at a ceremony in Warton to the Ministry of Defense on June 30, 2003, and the 17th (Reserve) Squadron began to fly Typhoon in January 2004. The model received its operational certification (RTS) on May 13, 2004, eliminating the operational restrictions imposed by the White Case. On November 4, 2005, the 29 (Reserve) Squadron was formed as an operational conversion unit at RAF Coningsby. [Crown Copyright / MOD]

Typhoon Centurion at the RAF

The Royal Air Force of the United Kingdom (RAF, for its acronym in English) received its first Typhoon within the Centurion project in the middle of 2018.

Speaking at the company's facilities in Warton, in northern England, a senior program official said the first Typhoons that were modified to operate the BVRAAM air-to-air missile (air-to-air missile beyond visual range) MBDA Meteor and the Storm Shadow cruise missile have been returned to their operating units, before the capacity is officially authorized for use in 2019.

"There are 26 aircraft now in the first phase of the Centurion Project standard, and the pilots started training in a few weeks," Eurofighter Director Andy Flynn said, adding, "Now we have to go through the approval process, which It should be finished by the end of the year (2018). "

The Centurion project configuration is intended to combine the already delivered Raytheon Paveway IV guided bomb, and the Storm Shadow, Meteor and Brimstone missiles in the Typhoon FGR4 in time for the RAF Panavia Tornado GR4 service withdrawal in March. 2019. The first phase of the aircraft that is delivered has been equipped with the Typhoon Phase 2 Enhancement (P2E) upgrade that includes the Meteor and Storm Shadow. Phase 2 of the Centurion Project covers the improvement of Phase 3 (P3E) of the Brimstone, and now the tests continue with this final configuration of the Centurion Project that began to be delivered to the RAF at the end of 2018.

The RAF has 51 Tranche 1, 67 Tranche 2 and approximately 29 of its 40 Typhoon planned Tranche 3. The Typhoons of Tranche 1 that will be retained will be used only in an air defense role and will not receive the update of the Centurion project .

A pair of Typhoon FGR4 of the RAF, the first one carries the logo of the centenary of this legendary air force. [Crown Copyright / MOD]

A Typhoon FGR4 during the trials of the Centurion program, the "triple racks2 for the Brimstone missiles are appreciated. [BAE]

A Typhoon FGR4 with a supersonic 1.000 liter tank and two ASRAAM missiles. [Crowsn copyright / MOD]

The Centurion project configuration is intended to combine the already delivered Raytheon Paveway IV guided bomb, and the Storm Shadow, Meteor and Brimstone missiles in the Typhoon FGR4 in time for retirement of the RAF service of the Panavia Tornado GR4 in March 2019. The first phase of the aircraft being delivered has been equipped with the Typhoon Phase 2 Enhancement (P2E) upgrade that includes the Meteor and Storm Shadow. Phase 2 of the Centurion Project covers the improvement of Phase 3 (P3E) of the Brimstone, and now the tests continue with this final configuration of the Centurion Project that began to be delivered to the RAF at the end of 2018. [Crown Copyright / MOD]

The RAF has 51 Tranche 1, 67 Tranche 2 and approximately 29 of its 40 Typhoons planned for Tranche 3. The Typhoons of Tranche 1 that will be retained will be used only in an air defense role and will not receive the Centurion project update. [BAE]

however 24 assigned to the Royal Saudi Air Force they were not replaced) and 40 of Tranche 3A.

These aircraft would equip five first-line squadrons (with 12 aircraft each), an operational conversion unit (OCU) and an operational evaluation unit (OEU). The 2015 defense and security strategic review indicated that two additional squadrons would be formed using Tranche 1 aircraft. One will be based on RAF Lossiemouth in Moray starting in 2019. More recently it has been known that a third squadron has been considered . However, everything depends on what can be "stretched" the defense budget.

The Typhoon entered service with the RAF under an agreement called "White Case", in which the manufacturer, BAE Systems provided 1,040 departures (1,300 flight hours) for the conversion of pilots and tests and operational evaluations from its aerodrome f Warton, using the new Tranche 1 Batch 1 of the RAF.

The first RAF plane, license plate ZJ803, was delivered at a ceremony in Warton to the Ministry of Defense on June 30, 2003, and the 17 (Reserve) Squadron began flying the Typhoon in January 2004.

The model received its operational certification (RTS) on May 13, 2004, eliminating the operational restrictions imposed by the White Case. On November 4, 2005 he was formed at RAF Coningsby on the 29th (Reserve) Squadron. The first Typhoon operational squadron was the 3 (Fighter) Squadron, reactivated at Coningsby on April 1, 2006, followed by the XI Squadron on March 29, 2007

The first operational tasks of the 3 (F) Squadron began on June 29, 2007, when it assumed the alarm service (QRA) of the south of the United Kingdom. On April 1, 2008 the squadron was declared to NATO as deployable in advanced air defense.

The XI Squadron was the leader for the RAF in providing air-surface attack capability. The first two Typhoon Block 5 (designated in the RAF as FGR4 and T3, the two-seater, on August 6, 2007.

The RAF received its first Tranche 2 in October 2008, when several were delivered to Coningsby. Four equipped the 1435 Flight (squadron) in the Falkland Islands, beginning the QRA alarms in September 2009. The Tranche 2 were mainly used to equip the third and fourth squadrons, being activated in RAF Leuchars. The 6 Squadron on September 6, 2010, assuming responsibility for the northern QRA on January 2, 2011. It also devoted itself to expanding the attack capabilities and versatility of the Tranche 2. The fourth operational squadron, 1 (F) Squadron it was reactivated in Leuchars on September 15, 2012, and the fifth II (Army Cooperation) Squadron on April 1, 2015, by which time the Scotland-based squadrons had moved to Lossiemouth, between May and September of 2014.

In December 2015, BAE Systems announced an order from the Sultanate of Oman for 12 Typhoon de la Tranche 3A (nine single-seaters and three two-seaters). The first two two - both tandem - flew for the first time from Warton on November 25, 2017, beginning in early 2018 deliveries to Silah al-Jaww Sultany 'Uman (Royal Air Force of Oman) where he has equipped the 8 Squadron in Thumrait, which until 2014 operated the Jaguar. [BAE]

Another new unit was released when the 17 Squadron was temporarily deactivated (to return equipped with F-35), and the important task of testing and evaluation for the Typhoon fell to the 41 Squadron in Coningsby.

Since 2014 the Typhoons operate in rotations in the operations against ISIS in Iraq and Syria, deployed in RAF Akrotiri, Cyprus.

The RAF is receiving the last of its 40 Tranche 3A, the first carrying out its initial flight on December 2, 2013. The last RAF squadron to receive the Typhoon is the IX (B) Squadron, which on April 1 was reactivated with Tranche 1 in RAF Lossiemouth, Scotland, taking the traditions and distinctive of the NO IX (B) Squadron equipped with Tornado GR4 that had been deactivated the previous day in RAF Marham.

Kuwait and Qatar

Following the confirmation in December 2017 by BAE Systems that Qatar had signed an order for 24 Eurofighter Typhoons, the Ministry of Defense of the United Kingdom revealed the details of a training package. Meanwhile, Eurofighter reported that the final production of the 28 aircraft ordered by Kuwait in 2016 is underway, and that they would be "the most advanced variant of the fighter aircraft ever manufactured."

The Qatar contract extends the final production line at BAE's Warton facilities, which were running out, until the 2020s. BAE said the contract has an approximate value of £ 5 billion ($ 6.8 billion)) and is still "subject to financing conditions", with the first payment scheduled for mid-2018, and which was delayed by two months. But the Ministry of Defense gave a value of "around £ 6 billion" for what it described as "the largest export agreement for the Typhoon project in a decade."

Deliveries will not start until the end of 2022, which may give enough time for them to train enough Qatari pilots and specialists to fly and maintain the aircraft, when the country's air force is also trying to absorb the 36 Dassault Rafale and 36 Boeing F -15QA Strike Eagle who also ordered. BAE Systems said it will "establish a new technical training school in Doha, focused on providing students with the critical skills necessary to support the air platforms of the Qatari Armed Forces in the future."

The Ministry of Defense said that a new "joint squadron" would be established at the Typhoon training base of the Royal Air Force, in Coningsby, with the reactivated No 12 Squadron, which took the designation of a newly disabled Tornado GR4 squadron, the who will be in charge of the instruction of the pilots of the Emirate of Qatar. The squad will "temporarily integrate Qatar personnel, including pilots and ground crew," the Defense Ministry added. It will operate some of the Typhoon Tranche 1 that the RAF previously planned to deactivate, but that in 2017 it changed its mind and decided to retain them.

The Kuwaiti aircraft are being assembled in the Leonardo production line in Italy and will be

Carrier Eurofighter

Presented at Aero India 2011, Eurofighter and BAE Systems provided for the first time more details about the studies carried out for the initial definition of the navalized Typhoon version.

These studies included the evaluation of the required design changes, simulations with pilots to redefine the aircraft's control and maneuverability capabilities and meetings with key suppliers. These studies indicated that these changes were possible, and would lead to the development of a first-class onboard fighter.

The most important element of the navalized Typhoon project was its exceptional weight-push relationship that would allow the aircraft to take off from an aircraft carrier without using a catapult, for which it would need the much simpler and more economical "ski-jump". The simulations showed that he would be able to take off in this way with a full charge of armament and fuel.

There would be few modifications necessary to make the Typhoon an onboard fighter and would include a reinforced landing gear, modified braking hook and reinforcements in some sections of the fuselage near the landing gear, as well as certain improvements in the EJ200 engines, which in order to reduce the speed of approach would be the version with vector thrust nozzles, which have already been tested by Eurojet, and which would be integrated into the advanced flight control system (FCS), allowing the pilot to fly the approach path while that he
the position of the nozzles of the motors.

The drawings shown in this box correspond to a Typhoon with the colors of the Indian Naval Aviation, which could have been to be your launch client. In principle Eurofighter has abandoned this project, which however would have been very interesting.

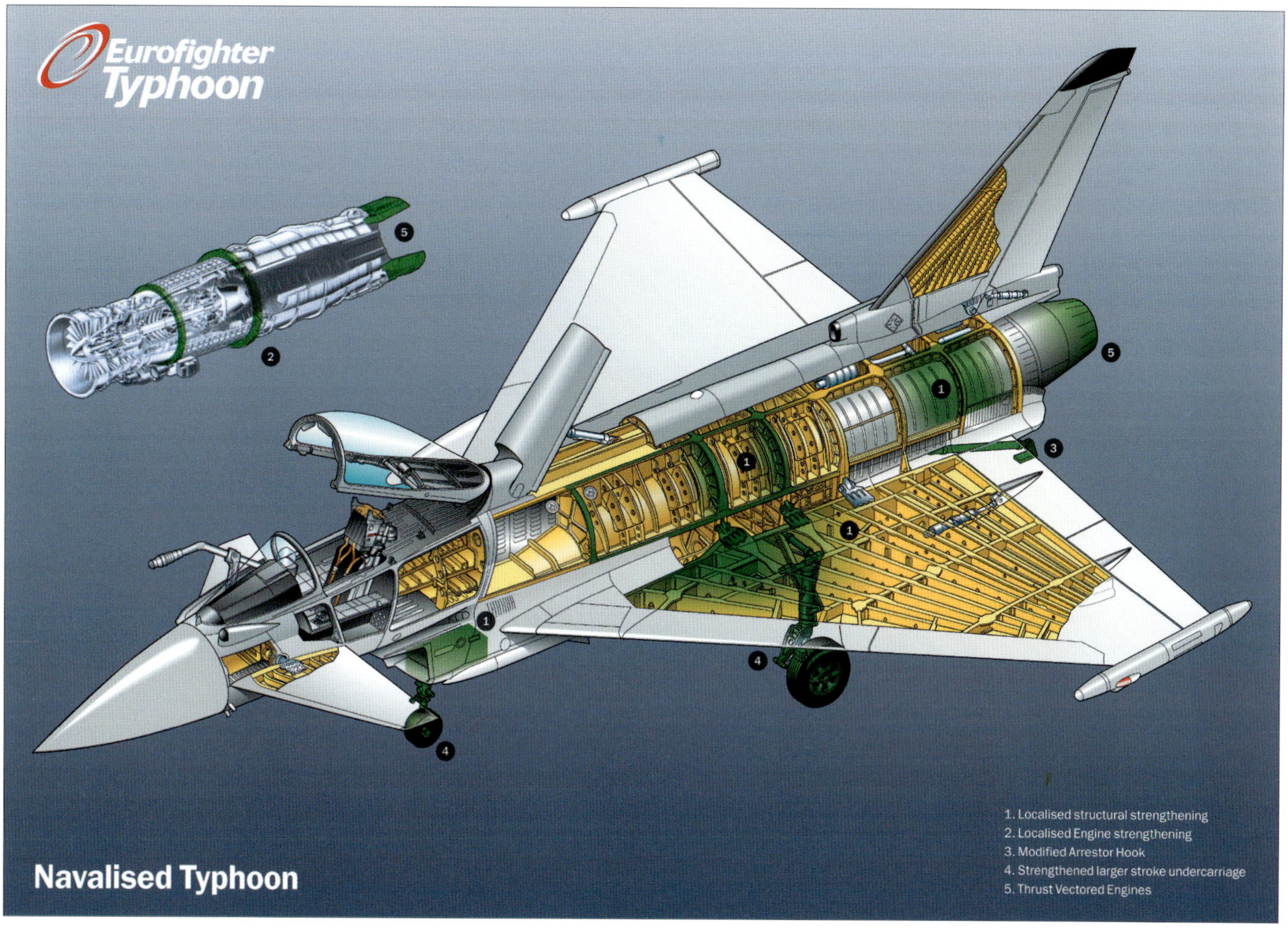

[Eurofighter]

Like any modern combat aircraft, the Eurofigther has many systems, of which the FCS of the "Carefree Handling" type developed by BAE Systems and GEC Marconi, which controls the maneuvers of the aircraft as well as other minor subsystems, should be highlighted. , like the admission of air through the varicrowl system. [José Manuel Martínez Álvarez]

the first ones built with the Captor E-Scan radar (AESA). The four original partner countries of Eurofighter have paid for the development of this radar, and a prototype was launched for the first time almost 10 years ago.

Leonardo stated that the Lockheed Martin Sniper laser designation pod has been integrated into the Kuwait Eurofighter, as well as the DRS-Cubic ACMI P5 combat training pod. The fighters will be equipped with the MBDA Storm Shadow and Brimstone plus "other surface-to-air weapons," the company added.

The agreement with the Ministry of Defense of Kuwait also includes the design and construction of the infrastructure at the Al-Salem air base; a set of training devices to establish an operational conversion unit there; and initial support services for three years (with an option for five others). Deliveries will be made from 2022 to 2024.

The ECR 90 Captor radar is based on the Radar Ferranti Blue Vixen of the Sea Harrier FA2, since the pulse frequency of the Fox Hunter radar of the Tornado F3 did not meet the requirements of the aircraft. The radar is of the fourth generation multimode type, with X-band Doppler pulse, which allows to identify targets over 150 km (BVR) and with search and lock capability up and down. The substitution of the mechanical scanning antenna with an AESA (Active Electronically Scanned Array) electronic scanning antenna of approximately 1,400 TR modules is planned as a radar upgrade. In this way, the radar will be called CAESAR (acronym for Captor AESA Radar). According to the Euroradar consortium (manufacturer of Euroradar CAPTOR) the capabilities of the Captor radar are significantly increased with the adoption of the electronic scanning antenna. Furthermore, according to this information, a Captor radar can be converted in a relatively simple way in CAESAR simply by changing the antenna and updating the software associated with the radar. [Euroradar]

Sensors

Like any modern combat aircraft, the Eurofigther has many systems, of which the FCS of the "Carefree Handling" type developed by BAE Systems and GEC Marconi, which controls the maneuvers of the aircraft as well as other minor subsystems, such as the admission, stand out. of air through the varicrowl system.

Captor-Caesar

The ECR 90 Captor radar is based on the Ferranti Blue Vixen of the Sea Harrier FA2, since the pulse frequency of the Fox Hunter radar of the Tornado F3 did not meet the requirements of the aircraft. The radar is of the fourth generation multimode type, with X-band Doppler pulse, which allows to identify targets over 150 km (BVR) and with search and lock capability up and down. As an improvement to the radar, the replacement of the mechanical scanning antenna with an electronic scanning antenna AESA (Active Electronically Scanned Array) of approximately 1,400 TR modules is foreseen. In this way, the radar will be called CAESAR (acronym for Captor AESA Radar). According to the Euroradar consortium (manufacturer of Euroradar CAPTOR) the capabilities of the Captor radar are significantly increased with the adoption of the electronic scanning antenna. Furthermore, according to this information, a Captor radar can be converted in a relatively simple way in CAESAR simply by changing the antenna and updating the software associated with the radar.

The PIRATE system (Passive Infra-Red Airborne Track Equipment) is an infrared tracking and tracking system (IRST) that is mounted on the left side of the Typhoon fuselage, in front of the windshield. [Ala11]

Dass

It is a system for detecting and responding to threats. The system warns of the presence of hostile activity and automatically activates the most appropriate countermeasures for each type of threat. The electronic helmet has a visor integrated in that provides information to the pilot regarding targets, speeds and distances.

The helmet's HST subsystem allows to target at what he/she is looking at, even if it is outside of the HUD's range of vision. Even being able to launch missiles at targets located "over the shoulder".

The DVI (Direct Voice Input) is a system that allows the interaction with the plane by means of the voice. The pilot can perform actions such as target assignments, navigation route changes, change of information on data presentation screens, etc.

The ESM system measures electromagnetic emissions and allows them to be identified, as well as their signatures.

In the cockpit there is a Head-Up-Display (HUD) with a wide field of vision in which information about the flight characteristics and combat modes is received, as well as images of the FLIR system of the PIRATE (see more ahead).

The Typhoon has three multifunction screens MHDD with all kinds of information. The controls follow the HOTAS doctrine containing more than 50 functions.

Praetorian

This fighter employs a sophisticated and highly integrated subsystem of defensive aids or DASS for its acronym in English (Defensive Aids Sub-System) called Praetorian, formerly EuroDASS. The Praetorian includes a radar alert receiver (RWR), a missile approach alert (MAW) and a laser alert receiver as threat detectors.

It also includes electronic countermeasure protection (ECM), chaff, flares and a towed radar decoy (TRD: Towed Radar Decoy). The Praetorian can automatically control and respond to any type of threat by providing the pilot with a full priority assessment of air-to-air and surface-to-air threats. It can respond to single or multiple threats.

The aircraft also has an advanced ground proximity warning system (GPWS) based on the reference TERPROM terrain navigation system used by the Panavia Tornado but even more advanced and fully integrated with the screens and cockpit controls. In the event that the pilot loses control of the plane, there is a pushbutton that when pressed makes the jet stabilize in straight and level flight.

MIDS

The MIDS (Multifunctional Information Distribution System) digital data transmission system provides the data link to the NATO Link 16 standardized information network used to exchange tactical information (such as flight paths, objectives, position, status and orders) between different units or military platforms in joint or combined missions.

IRST Pirate

The PIRATE system (Passive Infra-Red Airborne Track Equipment) is an infrared tracking system (IRST) that is mounted on the left side of the Typhoon fuselage, in front of the windshield. The Italian-British company SELEX Galileo is the main contractor, which together with the French company Thales Optronics and Tecnobit España, make up the EUROFIRST consortium responsible for the design and development of the system.

The Eurofighter employs a sophisticated and highly integrated defensive aids subsystem or DASS for its acronym in English (Defensive Aids Sub-System) called Praetorian, formerly EuroDASS. The DASS includes as threat detectors, a radar alert receiver (RWR), a missile approach alert (MAW) and a laser alert receiver. It also includes electronic countermeasure protection (ECM), chaff, flares and a towed radar decoy (TRD: Towed Radar Decoy). The Praetorian can automatically control and respond to any type of threat by providing the pilot with a full priority assessment of air-to-air and surface-to-air threats. It can respond to single or multiple threats. [S. Mafé)]

The Rafael Litening III (in Spain the associated company is Tecnobit) is the latest generation of this popular designator / illuminator for guided weapons, the previous variant, the Litening II equips the EF-18M Hornets of the Air Force and AV-8B + Harriers of the Navy. The current model incorporates numerous improvements, such as higher resolution in its day and night camera TV, as well as the infrared sensor (FLIR), also has more modes of designation, and also air-to-air function. In 2016 the CLAEX (Logistics Center for Armament and Experimentation) successfully completed the integration of Litening III into the Typhoon, twelve pods were purchased for Alas 11 and 14, while in 2019 it will receive another dozen of the most advanced Litening III Gen. 5

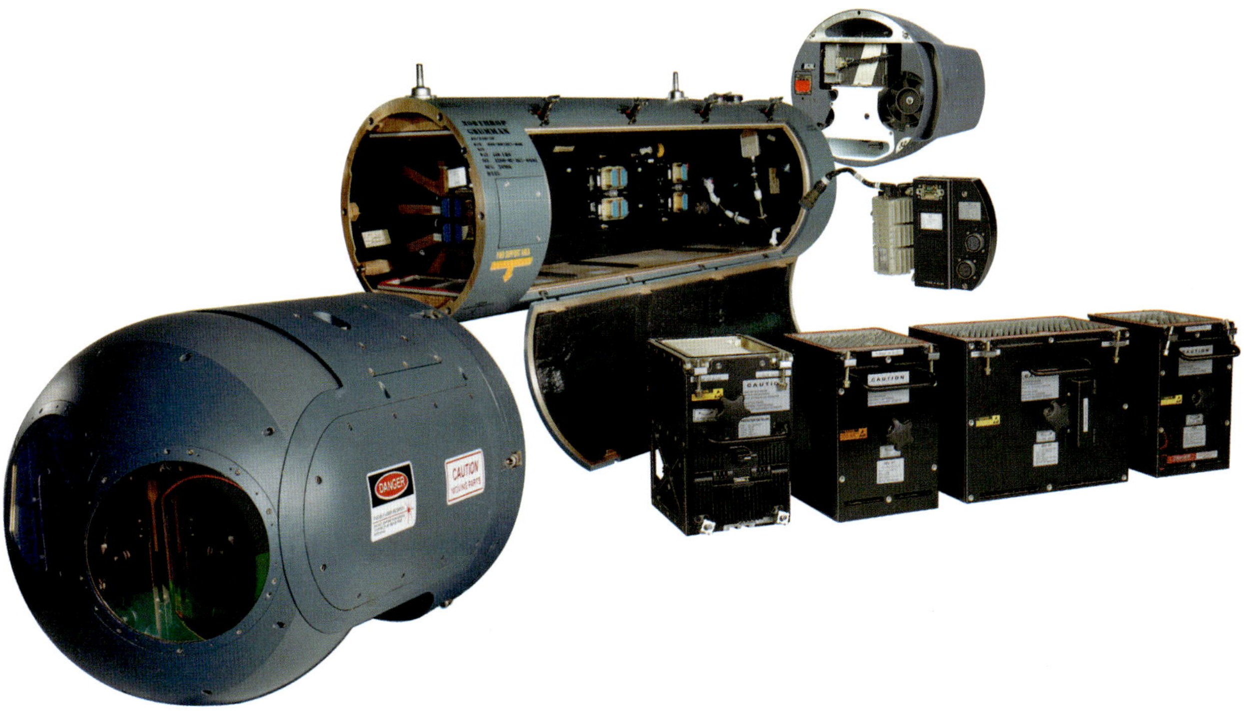

Chaff and flare dispensers are part of the DASS. [S. Mafé]

The PIRATE works in two bands of infrared radiation, 3-5 and 8-11 micrometers. When used in conjunction with the radar in an air-to-air mission, it functions as an infrared tracking system (IRST), providing detection and tracking of targets in passive mode. In an air-surface mission, it performs identification and location of objectives. It also provides navigation and landing assistance. It is linked to the viewer mounted on the pilot's helmet.

The Eurofighter began to incorporate the PIRATE in Block 5 of Tranche 1, the first being an example delivered to the Aeronautica Militare Italiana in August 2007. Anyway it can be achieved more advanced search capabilities with the addition of a targeting pod of objectives such as the Litening III or III Gen.5 (the latter of new generation). Or the French Damocles pod (as fitted to the Saudi, Omani, Qatari and Kuwaiti Typhoons)

Rafael Litening III / V

It is the latest generation of this popular designator / illuminator for guided weapons, is an advanced variant of the Litening II that equips the EF-18M Hornets of the Air Force and AV-8B+ Harriers of the Navy. The current model incorporates numerous improvements, such as higher resolution in its day and night camera TV, as well as the infrared sensor (FLIR), also has more modes of designation, and also air-to-air function. In 2016 the CLAEX (Logistics Center for Armament and Experimentation) successfully completed the integration of Litening III into the Typhoon, being acquired twelve examples for Alas 11 and 14, while in 2020 it will receive another dozen of the most advanced Litening III Gen. 5, also known as Litening V. This is a new standard of targeting pod — Litening V — is being integrated onto the aircraft which follows on from the current Litening III. It's being introduced to counter the increased threats that require operating at a greater standoff range to the target area and

The Eurofighter Typhoon has a single-tube 27 mm Mauser BK-27 cannon with a cadence of 1,700 rounds per minute, installed on the starboard side next to the wing root, with a capacity of 150 projectiles without tape, which are housed in a tank located in the center of the fuselage. [S. Mafé]

The IRIS-T missile, manufactured by the German company DBD, has a warhead of two-layer fragmentation of HE (High Explosive) and is equipped with an infrared imager (IIR) of 128 x 128 elements with ± 90 degrees of viewing angle on the pitch and roll axes. [Luftwaffe]

The flight control is done through the actuators that activate the tail fins and the gas orientation control of the rocket motor nozzle that allows turns with accelerations of up to 50 g. The two phases of the engine allow very sharp course changes after launch, improving their effectiveness against targets that move at high speed. [S. Mafé]

which require the best possible sensors. Litening V is also useful for night operations when its technological superiority can be best leveraged. The better the sensors, the better the image quality and the easier it is for the pilot to operate effectively in the darkness. The other evolutionary benefit of the new pod is processing power. As well as providing enhanced tracking of multiple moving ground targets, it can also be used for tracking multiple air tracks. This aspect is becoming more and more relevant as we move into a more congested, contested and low observable battlespace.

[MBDA]

AIM-2000 IRIS-T main features	
Range	12 km
Weight	21 kg
Dimensions (length / diameter)	1.80 / 0.09 m.
Two-Stage Solid Fuel Rocket Engines	
IIR guidance system	

Weapons

Cannon - The internal armament consists of a powerful 27 mm single-tube Mauser BK-27 cannon with a cadence of 1,700 rounds per minute, installed on the starboard side, next to the wing root. This weapon is provided in the Spanish, German, Italian and export aircraft while England, in a decision that raised many controversies, decided to initially dispense with it, considering the missiles as sufficient weapons. This attitude seems a repetition of the American decision, previous to the years of the conflict in Vietnam, who also assumed that the missile was the absolute weapon. Subsequent events forced the rapid installation of the cannon as complementary weaponry. The cannon has 150 linkless, which are housed in a magazine located in the center of the fuselage.

Air-air missile AIM-2000 IRIS-T - The program contemplates the acquisition of 700 short-range air-to-air missiles, plus 68 training to equip the Typhoon and F-18M Hornet fighter aircraft, through an international cooperation project .

The aim of the program is to provide the Air Force with a new generation short-range air-to-air missile (12 km) that will replace the AIM-9JULI / L / M Sidewinder missile series in the medium term.

Spain (20.9%), Germany (40.6%), Italy (14.8%), Greece (10.4%), Sweden (8.4%) and Norway (5.0%) participate in the program.). The deliveries of the missiles have occurred between the years 2007-2018.

The main contractor is the German company DBD (formerly BGT). The company SENER has been selected by DBD as a Spanish industrial partner in the program, being responsible for the manufacture of the actuators of the missile flight control system. Other Spanish companies also participate, such as EXPAL (manufacture of rocket engine elements) and ICSA (production of missile containers).

The IRIS-T missile manufactured by the German company DBD, has a warhead of fragmentation of two layers of HE (High Explosive) and is equipped with infrared imager search (IIR)

The AIM-120B AMRAAM is a version developed for export only through the US AMRAAM Product Enhancement program. It has a new digital processor, an erasable memory and programmable read only (EPROM) and five improved electronic units. [Raytheon]

of 128 x 128 elements with ± 90 degrees of angle of vision in the axes of pitch and roll.

The control of flight is made through the actuators that drive the tail fins and the control of gas orientation of the nozzle of the rocket motor that allows turns with accelerations of up to 50 g. The two phases of the engine allow very sharp course changes after launch, improving their effectiveness against targets that move at high speed.

The IRIS-T has been developed by a seven-nation team consisting of Germany, Canada, Spain, Greece, Italy, Norway and Sweden. The missile has been designed based on the dimensions of the Sidewinder, in its same mass and center of gravity, but it has two important innovations. One is the incorporation of vectorized thrust to give it great maneuverability and the second is a great capacity for launching with a large angle of deviation in relation to the sight line. Another peculiar characteristic of this missile is that of having four large fixed fins and some lines in relief along the fuselage, whose function is to provide lift and extend the range in a straight line in combination with the vectorized thrust. To allow its use in non-digitized old aircraft such as the Tornado or the Phantom, a connector for analog systems has been maintained, while for modern aircraft, such as the Eurofighter, they have a complete digital integration. Bodenseewerk Geratetechnik (BGT) has developed an entirely new search head that uses a device in the focal plane combined with a mechanical linear scanning mirror. The seeker head is mounted in a cradle that allows it to roll and pitch with a locking angle of +/- 90°. The development of the software and the digital signal processor are due to Saab. The search engine has proved effective during the tests carried out on a Sidewinder, achieving blockades against small drones in face confrontations, at distances of more than 5 km (3.1) miles and a deviation angle greater than 50°. The launch tests against targets from F-4 of the Luftwaffe, confirmed the goodness of the search engine.

The initial operational capacity was achieved in 2004. Production is expected to reach 4,000 units, of which Germany and Sweden must acquire most.

AIM-120 AMRAAM

The AIM-120 developed by Hughes is now owned by Raytheon and is the western exponent of the missiles to be used beyond visual range and the only one that has been used in combat.

Its eternal appearance is very similar to the AIM-7 Sparrow and both missiles are approximately the same length. The AMRAAM is thinner, lighter has smaller guiding fins and a larger radome. The AMRAAM was the first air-to-air missile with an active radar search engine that allowed it to search its targets independently, once

The most differentiating features of the METEOR are two asymmetrical air intakes for the ramjet, a pair of fins mounted in the middle of the fuselage and four later. The asymmetry of the air intakes has been adopted to avoid that in very tight maneuvers they can be in "aerodynamic shadow", causing the "blackout" of the engine due to lack of air. In addition, the engine has a sophisticated combustion system for fuel and hot gas to avoid the flame-out (engine stop). [MBDA]

Next to the main landing gear, the Eurofighter carries chaff and flare dispensers. [S. Mafé]

those were within range. The AMRAAM still needs the launch plane for initial priming and middle course guidance. To achieve this, discrete energy packets are transmitted in the X-band, using the side lobes to update the missile's target position. The use of these lateral waves, these lateral lobes (is a characteristic of propagation of radar emissions in which part of the radiated energy is separated from the main beam of emission), the launching plane can turn around, allowing it to be put out of reach of the possible answer. A conventional missile requires the launch plane to maintain its course, which is more or less straight to the target, approaching it to a dangerous distance. Conversely, when the AMRAAM is guided by data link in its middle course, the launch plane may turn around but still have to keep the target within the boundary of the articulated cradle of the radar antenna (horizontal blocking angle), to maintain coverage with the side lobes. In the guiding terminal phase, the missile activates its own search radar and the launch plane is free to maneuver completely off-stage. The AMRAAM has a range of 50 km (31 miles) but the range of its radar is less. It is a highly classified figure that is believed to be approximately 10 km (6.2 miles).

C.16 of the 111 Squadron launching its load of flares. [Ignacio Núñez]

The AIM-120B is a version developed for export only through the US AMRAAM Product Enhancement program. It has a new digital processor, an erasable memory and programmable read only (EPROM) and five improved electronic units.

Spain has already confirmed that for the future it will install the version AIM-120C-5/7 in its Eurofighter, EF-18M Hornet and AV-8B Plus.

It has a Plus 5 rocket engine, a warhead of fragmentation and the fins cut to adapt it to the holds of the F-22 and the F-35. The new engine is faster than existing rockets, so it increases the possibility of survival and its scope. The rocket motor, which is 12.7 cm longer, has been accommodated by redesigning and modifying the size of the actuator of the rear wings. In this way the C-5 maintains the same weight, centering and dimensions of the other variants.

Another important aspect of this missile is its reliability, which can be measured in thousands of hours. The production missiles, which are flying daily in the air forces of 24 countries, have demonstrated 1,500 hours between failures.

MBDA METEOR

As of 2018/2019 the AIM-120 missile will begin to be replaced / complemented by the Meteor for use beyond the visual range (BVRAAM). This missile is selected to meet the requirements of the RAF known as SR (A) 1239 and is built by a consortium, basically European, led by MBDA and BAE Systems with the participation of Alenia Marconi Systems, LFK, Airbus Military, Saab and Boeing This last company is mainly involved in the integration of the weapon and marketing. The Meteor was preferred to the FMRAAM offered by Raytheon as an alternative, after a strong competition. It is a fourth-generation missile, with the pretense of being effective beyond 100 km (62 miles). The great novelty is that the rocket motor has been replaced by a strangleable ramjet, produced by Bayern-Chemie and that has been in development since 1990. The most differentiating characteristics of the projectile are two asymmetrical air intakes for the ramjet, a pair of fins mounted in the middle of the fuselage and four later. The asymmetry of the air intakes has been adopted to avoid that in very tight maneuvers they can be in "aerodynamic shadow", causing the "blackout" of the engine due to lack of air. In addition, the engine has a sophis-

Eurofighter Typhoon of Ala14 in which an AIM-2000 IRIS-T, GBU-48 and Meteor can be seen. [AMRAAM]

[MBDA]

Operational advantages of the Meteor:

Effective operational capacity in all environmental conditions; guided by an active radar search engine, the Meteor provides all-weather capability to combat a variety of targets. Designed to meet the most stringent requirements in the harshest environments. The Meteor gives the pilot an outstanding ability to "hook".

Capacity for use in network (network); This ability to operate in a network, communicating through the data link, allows it to operate using data from the target provided by third parties, allowing the pilot the most flexible air-air weapons system that exists today.

It has the largest lethal capacity in existence due to the combination of its characteristics, ramjet propulsion system, solid fuel, rocket with vectorial thrust.

Complete destruction of the target; equipped with impact and proximity fuze, plus an explosive warhead / fragmentation, to maximize its lethality.

Technical characteristics and specifications	
Weight:	190 kg.
Length:	3.7 m
Diameter:	178 mm.
Ejection capacity by ejection and from pylon.	
Propulsion:	Vector push rocket engine (ramjet) with solid fuel.
Search engine:	active RF.
Navigation and guidance:	inertial middle course with data link, guided autonomous terminal.
Warhead:	explosive / fragmentation.
Fuzes, impact, RF proximity.	

[TAURUS GMBH]

Missile KEPD-350 TAURUS

The TAURUS cruise missile program, also called ALAD, provides the Air Force with a long-range air-surface missile (approximately 300 km) against specific high-value targets for the Eurofighter Typhoon and Boeing EF-18M Hornet fighters. . The KEPD-350 TAURUS missile, manufactured by TAURUS GMBH, is capable of flying completely autonomous once launched from the aircraft. During the flight, it is guided by its Triple Function Navigation System: Inertial Navigation System (IMS), GPS capable of receiving and processing signals in C / A frequencies (commercial use) and P / Y (military use), and System of Navigation by Land Reference and Based on Images, which makes the navigation more precise.

Specifications	
Weight	1,400 kg
Length	5.1 m
Diameter	1.08 m
Effective range	500 km
Warhead	500 kg
Engine	Williams P8300-15
Width	2,064 m
Low level altitude	30-40 m
Maximum speed	0.85 - 0.95 mach
Guidance system	IBN (Image Based Navigation), INS (Inertial Navigation System), TRN (Terrain Referenced Navigation) and MIL-GPS (Global Positioning System)

[MBDA]

Missile MBDA Brimstone New Design

A fighter aircraft armed with the Brimstone missile offers range, speed, speed, flexibility, precision and the ability to hook multiple targets with a single mission charge. The Brimstone offers a quick response to the requirements of close air support (CAS) and counterinsurgency operations.

The system can be operated in three modes, each equipped with great flexibility:

Mode 1: semiactive laser guidance (SAL), for pawning static targets without a radar signature or a very low one. (RCS).

Mode 2: guided SAL and millimeter radar wave, for fast targets or located in a confused environment.

Mode 3: Pawn multiple targets simultaneously in fire and forget mode.

The Brimstone has been integrated into the Typhoon of the RAF, in triple launchers; the Air Force has identified one in need of a weapon of this type, that is, light, of great precision and of course little or no collateral damage, and possibly in the near future this missile was acquired to equip its Typhoon squadrons.

Specifications	
Weight	48.5 kg
Length	1.8 m
Diameter	0,178 m
Effective range	12 km
Solid fuel rocket engine	
Spread	0.3 m
Maximum speed	1,3-1,5 mach
Guidance system	Inertial navigation system (INS) or radar

[MBDA]

Missile MBDA SPEAR (Selective Precision Effects At Range)

Basically it is a Brimstone with steroids, that is to say a mini cruise missile and is the answer to a requirement formulated by the British Ministry of Defense known as Selective Precision Effects At Range (SPEAR). Recent conflicts have demonstrated the need for precision weapons that can operate under any conditions, and in an environment of severe countermeasures, attacking targets in movement and maneuvering. Propelled by a small reactor and equipped with planes, the SPEAR has a range beyond the horizon, ensuring that the carrier aircraft is out of reach of hostile anti-aircraft defenses.

The SPEAR will equip the British Typhoons (and F-35). The Air Force is studying it, because sometimes it is much more economical to beat an objective with an SPEAR than with one of the much more expensive Taurus, although at the time of writing these lines, there is no program for its evaluation / acquisition.

Specifications	
Weight	100 kg
Length	1,800 mm
Diameter	180 mm
Power plant jet engine	
Operating range	130/140 km
Guidance system	Control surfaces

[Sergio Ruiz González]

GBU-16 / GBU-48

Laser-guided bombs (LGB) were introduced in 1968 to meet the requirements of USAF precision guided pumps. Semi-active LGBs "fly" over the energy of the reflected laser beam directed at the target. The illumination of the target can be done by the launch aircraft, by a third aircraft or by ground troops operating a laser designator. The LGB are, in fact, a laser guide kit applicable to current conventional non-guided pumps.

Laser-guided bombs have reduced the number of weapons requested to destroy a single target while improving accuracy, reliability and profitability in attack missions. LGBs were introduced during Vietnam and then used in Panama, Iraq, the former Yugoslavia, Afghanistan, Libya and Syria. The USAF, US Navy and USMC and the air forces of 31 nations of the world have ordered Paveway bombs and more than 152,000 Paveway II kits have been produced to date.

The GBU-16 Paveway II consists of a 1,000 pound (500 kg) Mk 83 pump with an added laser guide package. It can address the same objectives committed by the GBU-10, but minimizing the potential collateral damage, since its guidance fins are progressive, while those of the GBU-10, are "all or nothing", ie maximum or zero Deflection

The Enhanced Paveway II EGBU-16 (also known as GBU-48) is a dual-mode guided pump designed to operate effectively in all-weather conditions. The laser-guided GBU-16 can only operate in optimal weather conditions, which endangers the laser beam that guides the pump through its intended target. The EGBU-16, which was introduced in 2001 during Operation Enduring Freedom in Afghanistan, is based on the semiactive laser guidance and the inertial guidance system assisted by the Global Positioning System (GPS) to achieve the goal without problems. The GPS guides the pump in adverse weather conditions and the laser guide helps the mobile targets of opportunity.

The EGBU-16 bomb was used successfully during the military operations in Afghanistan (Enduring Freedom 2001) and Iraq (Iraqi Freedom 2003) by the United States Air Force. The same weapon was selected by the armed forces of Spain, and is integrated into both the Eurofighter Typhoon and the F-18M Hornet.

[USAF]

GBU-39B

The Small Diameter Bomb (SDB - Small Diameter Bomb), is an all-weather weapon with a diurnal and nocturnal envelope composed of a 125 kg MK-81 body. Its small size allows the launch plane to carry more GBU-39B, making it possible to beat more targets and reduce the chances of collateral damage. It is not yet in service with the Spanish Typhoons, although it is supposed to be soon.

ticated combustion system for fuel and hot gas to avoid the flame-out (engine stop).

The Meteor is designed to equip not only the Eurofighter Typhoon of the RAF, but also the Swedish Gripen, the French Rafale, as well as the F-35B of the RAF/RN. It has also been adopted by the other partners of the Eurofighter program, in addition to Saudi Arabia, Qatar, Kuwait and Oman. Guidance is inertial and by data link in the middle trajectory and by means of a search radar during the final guidance until the impact. This radar is from Alenia Marconi.

In 2000, the acquisition budget of the United Kingdom for an unspecified amount of missiles

The Eurofighter flight gear does not maintain common elements with the rest of the equipment that equips the fighter units of the Spanish Air Force or another air force. [José M. Martínez]

amounted to 890 million Pounds. The program, which has suffered considerable delays that now reach thirteen years, has displaced the date of entry into service from 2005 to 2018, the year in which the first unit of Eurofighter already had 72 missiles and all their equipment support. Probably the most important consequence of the launching of this program is that the monopoly of technology "beyond visual range" is finally taken away from the United States, with the consequent advantages for Europe.

The Eurofighter pilot flight gear

The choice of the flight gear of the Eurofighter Typhoon pilot follows the model of most systems and subsystems of this aircraft, it was designed from scratch.

It was in response to the operational requirements initially established by the nations instead of following the traditional model, of integrating existing equipment and seats in the market, in the cockpit of a new airplane and adapting small national variants of it.

In the case of the Eurofighter and in view of the demanding requirements that users imposed on the system, the industry reviewed each of the elements of the personal flight equipment existing at that time in the market and discarded most of them, for not complying with the demands of the new weapons system, initiating new research and development programs, which have allowed advanced designs capable of satisfying the operational demands of the new aircraft. The incorporation of women into the collective of fighter pilots has also meant an innovation in design requirements that until now did not include any of the existing equipment.

The personal equipment of a pilot contributes to provide protection and is an essential element in the human-machine interaction:

In cold areas such as during Baltic Air Policing, the pilot wears the anti-exposure equipment, called "wet suit". It is a waterproof suit that keeps the body dry and forms a thermal capsule that allows the pilot to survive in case of ejection on water. [Christian Schack]

-Protection against external agents of the flight such as lack of oxygen, sudden depressurization or ejecting at high altitude (65,000 ft), the impact with birds, extreme temperatures, effects of gravity on the turns and solar radiation at great height.

-Protection in case of abandonment of the plane by emergency on land and in case of ejecting in flight. Protection against aggressive factors

Beginning with the flight suit and ending with the socks of the pilot, all the elements respond to a new design that mostly requires a total personalization to each individual's complexion, which it forces to multiply the sizes and complicates the logistics enormously. [Jorge Portalés]

The choice of the flight gear of the pilot of the Eurofighter Typhoon follows the pattern of most systems and subsystems of this aircraft, was designed from scratch. [Jorge Portalés]

such as impact with air and soil, smoke, fire and survival on land and sea.

-Protection against hostile agents of combat, such as the effect of enemy weapons, laser radiation, NBC agents (radioactive, chemical and biological).

-But in addition, the flight equipment is now an essential part of the man-plane interface, facilitating the exchange of information and data between the pilot and the on-board systems through the integrated viewfinder in the flight helmet and communications. Obvious examples are the presentation of infrared images, presentation of flight and mission data, visual designation of targets, voice command, and other functions associated, for example, with the flight helmet of the Eurofighter pilot.

-Protection and interface with the systems, are functions that must be made compatible with an essential requirement of the current fighter aircraft: persistence. A quality that allows them to fly for an unlimited time, thanks to the capacity of refueling in flight, oxygen regeneration systems and communications with AWACS or via satellite that allow to maintain command and control at distances from the theater of operations previously unthinkable. In these conditions the flight time of a fighter only has a limiting factor that is the physical resistance of the pilot, to which the design and comfort of his flight equipment contributes directly, which should favor his/her ability to move and provide maximum comfort for support during long missions of the order of eight or ten flight hours that in the last conflicts are considered normal.

A pilot of the 111 Squadron prepares for a training mission. [Jorge Portalés]

A unique gear in the air force, made by pilots for pilots

The flight crew of the Eurofighter does not maintain common elements with the rest of the equipment that equips the fighter units of the any of the using Air Forces. Starting with the flight suit and finishing with the pilot's socks and boots, all the elements respond to a new design that, in

The test pilot Alfonso de Castro, after the first flight with the IPA4, wears the helmet called ACS Helmet (Air Combat System). [Airbus]

its majority, requires a total customization of each individual's complexion. This forces to multiply the necessary sizes and enormously complicates the logistics. It is necessary to adapt each element exactly to the measures of the individual, with what its use becomes exclusive and therefore the exchange or use of existing elements is not possible. Additionally, all the components of the equipment have been designed as an integral set, which must adapt to each other by adding or subtracting layers, depending on the environmental conditions or threat. Details like allowing the pilot the ability to tie his boots, look back or be able to reach the parachute fittings even equipped with the maximum layers were considered essential from the beginning.

The development of the elements that constitute the flight gear of the Eurofighter has followed a model process where the user and the engineers responsible for the design have worked together facing the problems and solutions. The industry responsible for the equipment (BAE Systems) claimed from the beginning the cooperation of the four nations through a working group to which each country had to provide at least one expert in aerospace medicine, a test pilot and a pilot with operational experience. This group was initially responsible for clarifying with the industry the operational requirements of the user, the source of the majority of errors committed by design engineering and subsequently actively involved through periodic evaluations where prototypes of each of the elements The components that make up the equipment were tested and evaluated exhaustively, methodically and continuously, either in exact replicas of the cabin, in centrifugal chambers or aboard Hawk 100 aircraft, specially equipped to simulate the flight characteristics of the Typhoon. The Spanish Ejército del Aire included in this working group from the first moment, experts in aerospace medicine from CIMA (Center for Aerospace Medicine), pilots of CLAEX (Spanish AF Test Center) and pilots of units of F-18 and Mirage F1. The engineering component was contributed by INTA (Institute of Aerospace Technics) personnel and all of them together with their colleagues from other nations have made it possible to reach solutions to the problems that fully satisfy the aspirations of the pilot and the expectations of the industry.

A European industrial cooperation program

Like the rest of the equipment and systems of this aircraft, all those components subject to research and development were awarded through competition, to industrial consortiums with representation of the four nations in order to facilitate one of the basic rules of the Eurofighter program: guaranteeing the nations an industrial return proportional to the investment committed. In the case of Spain, its participation of 14% has allowed companies such as Parafly and official research centers such as INTA, to have been involved in the design, production, evaluation and certification of some elements of the team, in addition to share information related to the research and development activities of the whole.

The flying suit

Due to the strong pressures with which the anti-G suit works, it was necessary to design a lightweight flight suit, which minimized the number of zippers and folds affected by the anti-G pants. Its construction makes for an exhaustive use of Velcro. Two similar garments have been designed, although with different fabrics for summer and winter. Spain and Italy have opted for the summer option while Germany and Britain have been equipped in principle for the cold. The fabric is breathable, anti-allergic and includes a treatment that makes it resistant to fire and certain agents.

The anti-G equipment

The turning capacity of the Eurofighter, in combination with the power of its engines and its enormous weight-bearing ratio, means that in evasive maneuvers or combat maneuvers are reached and maintained for short periods, values

A pilot from Ala 14 prepares to carry out a training mission during the detachment of this unit in the Baltic Air Policing in 2016. [EA]

of severity of the order of 9 G. The human body is not designed to withstand 8 or 10 times the force of gravity and reacts initially to the loss of blood flow in the brain, with gray vision, loss of color, reduction of visual field or tunnel effect, loss of vision and finally loss of consciousness (G-LOC) that can last between 15 or 20 seconds and that occurring in the air, in a single-seat airplane, can have fateful consequences. The other factor that contributes negatively in the phenomenon of Gs forces is the rate at which they increase (G-onset). In an aircraft such as the Eurofighter, values close to 20 G per second can be achieved, which gives the pilot only 0.5 seconds of reaction to prepare his body before a sudden increase of 9 G, and it is the same time that the systems have of protection of the plane to act.

The operational requirements of the Eurofighter, and based on the experience accumulated with early fourth-generation aircraft, like the F-16 and F-18, required a protective equipment that freed the pilot from the risk of loss of consciousness. Additionally, the pilot must be able to maintain 9Gs without making any effort to counteract them. The existing anti-G systems are based on a pneumatic trouser that, by applying pressure to the abdomen and legs of the pilot, keeps the blood pressure concentrated in the head and upper body. The pilot must contribute to this mechanism by keeping air in his lungs and contracting the diaphragm which causes additional physical effort and contributes to exhaustion.

To facilitate this maneuver, the Eurofighter anti-G equipment and the US industry trends for the new generation of F-22 and F-35 aircraft with its "Combat Ace" equipment, include a forced breathing system, which injects air under pressure in the lungs of the pilot proportional to the number of G and a pectoral anti-G that like a vest is inflated simultaneously with the trousers, generating a pressure from the outside that compresses the chest, keeping the blood pressure in the upper body The trousers to get a greater effect, they are integral and they embrace the legs completely including the feet, that support the pressure of some air bags that swell inside the flight boots. The chest vest, the anti-G pants and the forced breathing, also work in case of depressurization of the cabin giving protection to the pilot up to 55,000 feet. The anti-G pectoral also integrates a very low profile collar type lifejacket with automatic opening, perfectly integrated in the shape of the vest as well as the arm retractors required by the new Mk16 ejection seat for the launch event.

The anti-G set has demanded, due to its complexity and innovative design, many hours of adjustments and tests. One of the problems that arose initially was the pain of the pilot's arms caused by the fact of being excluded from the pneumatic pressure of the suit, in order not to diminish their mobility and aggravated by the position of the seat and the controls of the airplane that place the forearms below the height of the heart. It was observed that to maintain an adequate blood pressure in the brain, it was necessary to accept a high pressure in the forearms, which resulted in the breakage of capillaries, bruises and intense pain in flight at the end of the maneuvers.

After many tests of the equipment in a centrifugal chamber and on an airplane, it was observed that a more balanced distribution of the pressures in each of the components of the anti-G equipment, managed to overcome the problem and now the equipment allows the pilot to accept without effort a number of Gs much higher than that normally supported in current aircraft, without physical contribution to the maneuver.

The anti-exposure equipment

Also called "wet suit". It is a waterproof suit that keeps the body dry and forms a thermal capsule that allows the pilot to survive in the case of ejecting over water at low temperatures. In flights over the ocean, rescue teams may need a minimum of 48 hours to locate the position and evacuate the pilot, bearing in mind that the range of action of a helicopter does not allow its use at certain distances from the coast. The use of an anti-exposure suit even in summer time in certain circumstances is mandatory.

The biggest drawback of the current suits is the discomfort produced by its rubber or nylon texture and the hermetic seals in the areas of wrists and collars. They are difficult to put on and take off so in advanced alarm states they require the pilot to stay on the ground with his suit on. The fact of not perspiring, together with its hermeticity causes sweating and the associated discomforts. In flight they are bulky, not very flexible and perspiration continues to be a problem.

The anti-exposure suit of the Eurofighter based on new "Gore-Tex" fibers, has the texture of a normal cotton fabric, pleasant to the touch, it is thin, breathable and totally waterproof. The zippers are also a new design, safer, easier to act and their arrangement greatly shortens the time needed to dress and undress. The fabric also includes treatments against chemical agents, fire and above all, cockpit comfort is much higher than the current suit.

The interior cooling equipment

The technology in the field of new microfibers has advanced a lot in the line of competitive sports and high mountain, today it is easy to get a pajama underwear, shirt and pants, has the same effect as the jacket and pants lined with skin back, which made up the cold team in Great Britain and Germany, to fly through northern Europe during WWII and after. The set was bulky, significantly restricted the mobility of the pilot and combined badly with the anti-G and anti-exposure suit. In the team of the Eurofighter, the torso can be combined with another garment type vest with short sleeves that duplicates the thermal effect of the set without providing just volume.

The interior warming equipment

The need to provide protection to the pilot anywhere in the world and in extreme weather conditions, together with the need to fly in the Eurofighter with an integral anti-G suit and the

Close-up of the electronic helmet called Helmet Mounted Symbology System (HMSS). [S. Mafé]

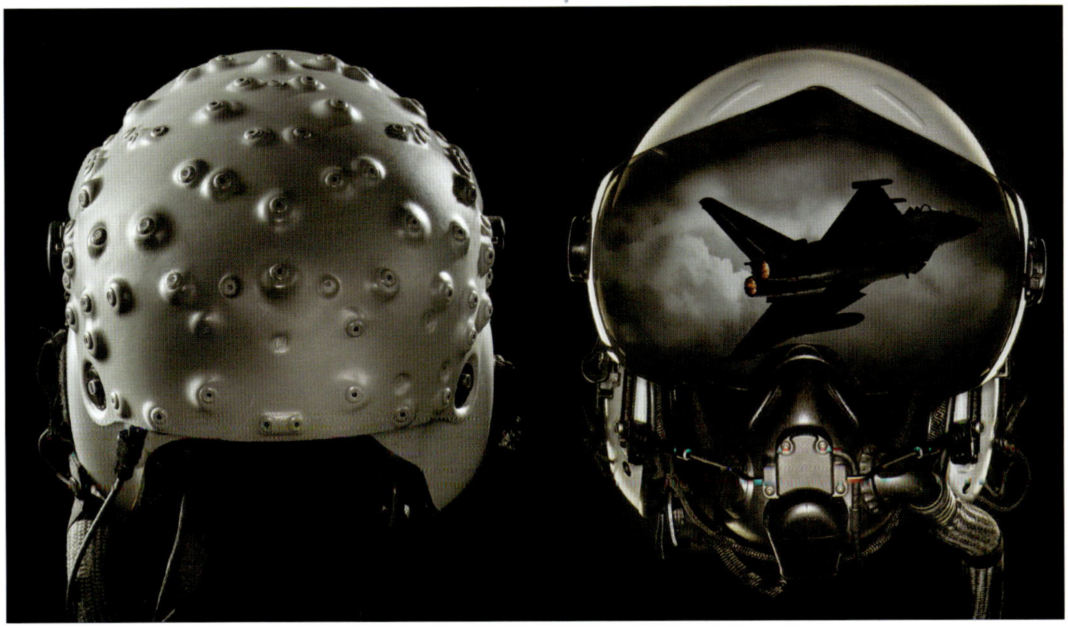

HMSS bulges are sensors that connect with others in the cockpit to provide the pilot with a perfect situational awareness. [BAE]

The pilot helmet

The real industrial challenge was to design a helmet that integrates in its viewer the possibility of presenting data, images, symbols with which to designate targets or aim weapons and night vision capability. All this while maintaining the physical protection provided by the traditional helmet and the most difficult, maintaining the centering and weight to support the 9G maintained. The resulting helmet, called the Helmet Mounted Symbology System (HMSS), if stripped of avionics equipment, is the lightest on the market with a better response to impact than most existing helmets. The helmet of the Eurofighter must protect the head and the face of the pilot against the physical impact, the impact of the wind in ejecting at high speed and the eyes of the glare or the action of a laser.

It is composed of two parts: An interior adjustment module, which adapts perfectly to the head of the pilot and must ensure its fixation without gaps, because the helmet now becomes a viewfinder and must form a part with the head of the pilot, to guarantee accuracy An external part, which adapts to the adjustment module and which can be considered an avionics device plus the airplane, which can be changed in the flight line, in the event of a breakdown. It contains two cathode ray tubes that can present on the pilot's visor, the images provided by the FLIR housed in the nose of the plane, the images of the night vision cameras integrated in the same helmet, flight parameters and tactical information from the navigation and attack system, as well as information from the Litening III, or simply a cursor with which to orient the weapons with just looking towards the target.

The UK's RAF Eurofighter Typhoon squadrons have a heavy workload, with QRA and Air Policing roles alongside operations like Op Shader, but despite this the maintenance record is close to perfect. It's a reliability record which is hugely impressive. Says Wing Commander O'Grady: "For me success on Op Shader was about making sure the Royal Air Force and in particular XI Squadron delivered what it is asked to deliver. That was getting jets airborne every day to fill the slots we're assigned to fill, providing coverage over the area we're supposed to be over at the right time. Then doing our job when called on — whether that's close air support, delivering kinetic effects to help the ground situation or armed over-watch in support of coalition forces both in Iraq and Syria. And do it all in a safe manner with no mistakes. Yes, my engineers work incredibly hard but ultimately the jet's really serviceable. I can't remember when we did an engine change because it broke, it just doesn't, the serviceability is exceptional." [Crown copyright/MoD]

thermal load that supposes having to support up to four daily missions, led to the conclusion that a classic system based on sweating/evaporation could bring dehydration problems to the pilot, so a liquid cooling system was considered. The conditioned suit consists of an inner vest cooled by a system of liquid ducts that surround the chest and back of the pilot and which is connected to the air conditioning system. During the journey to the jet on land, the pilot has a suitcase that, as a stand-alone device, allows him to keep the circulation of the cold liquid on the vest and thus avoid sweating and the sensation of heat.

Scramble!

Fighter jets from several NATO countries scrambled on Wednesday (11 March 2020) to intercept Russian military aircraft off the western coasts of Scotland and Ireland and over the Gulf of Biscay.

Allied Air Command through its two subordinate Combined Air Operations Centres (CAOCs) at Uedem, Germany, and Torrejon, Spain, conducted a consolidated response to Russian Federation Air Force planes flying in international airspace over the North Atlantic.

RAF quick reaction alert Typhoon aircraft from RAF Lossiemouth scrambled to monitor two Tu-142 Bear Maritime Patrol Aircraft bombers while they were in the UK area of interest on 11 March 2020. This was the second time RAF jets have been scrambled to monitor Russian aircraft in the last few days.

Air Chief Marshal Mike Wigston, Chief of the Air Staff, said:

'These Russian bombers do not comply with international air traffic rules, are a hazard to airliners and are not welcome in our airspace. RAF Typhoons, alongside our NATO allies, ensured these Russian aircraft posed no hazard.'

One of the Quick Reaction Alert pilots from RAF Lossiemouth, who intercepted the Russian Bears, said:

"This was my first time intercepting Russian Long Range Aviation and everything ran on rails. Our first intercept occurred to the west of the Shetland Islands, where we shadowed the two Russian Tu-142 Bear-F aircraft as they tracked south.

The UK has some of the busiest airspace in the world and civilian airliners are constantly using the airways in this area, so our presence ensured UK Air Traffic Controllers could continue to manage this busy airspace around the hazard of the Russian activity.

Subsequently the two Russian Bears continued to track south towards the Bay of Biscay where they were met by French Quick Reaction Alert. We intercepted the Bears as they turned back North before we handed them off to additional QRA Typhoons again launched from RAF Lossiemouth."

Two Russian Bear-F Tu-142 long range MPA approached from the North East and flew in international airspace off the West coast of the UK, down towards the Bay of Biscay, where French assets monitored them and then returned North. At no point did the Russian aircraft enter UK sovereign airspace.

Additional air to air refuelling support was provided by RAF Voyager aircraft from RAF Brize Norton alongside comms and radar support from the National Air and Space Operations Centre (High Wycombe) and Air Surveillance and Control System (RAF Boulmer). All of these elements remain on constant vigil to provide the RAF's contribution to the defence of the UK.

The primary role of the Royal Air Force is to defend the UK, 365, 24/7 and, when necessary, UK interests overseas; the RAF will continue to remain alert and ready to intercept any unidentified military or civilian aircraft around UK airspace.

Recent events have increased awareness of Russian military activity, however, the RAF have routinely intercepted, identified and escorted Russian air assets that transit international airspace within the UK's area of interest.

The primary role of the RAF is to control the air over the UK. Our impressive multi-role Typhoon fighter squadrons are based at RAF Coningsby, RAF Lossiemouth and in the Falkland Islands.

Today and every day they maintain the highest level of readiness. At home, under the direction of our controllers at RAF Boulmer (Northumberland) and Scampton (Lincolnshire) our fighters can be scrambled to intercept, identify and, if required, intervene unidentified aircraft approaching our shores. This is a routine part of the RAF's air defence role to protect UK airspace.

QRA are launched to intercept unidentified aircraft because the aircraft cannot be identified by any other means. i.e. the aircraft is not talking to civilian or military Air Traffic Control, has not filed a flight plan and is not transmitting a recognisable secondary surveillance radar code.

QRA procedures entail RAF aircraft and crews being held at continuous high readiness 24/7, so that they can take off within minutes to protect UK sovereign airspace. Aircraft are available at each base allowing us to provide good response across the country.

For the third time in a buy six days of March 2020, RAF Typhoon aircraft from RAF Lossiemouth and RAF Coningsby have been scrambled to intercept Russian long-range aircraft.

Two Russian Tupolev Tu-160 Blackjack strategic bombers approached the UK Flight Information Region (FIR), north of the Scottish coast before flying down the west coast of Ireland.

These scrambles have been caused by the Russian aircraft entering the UK FIR, the UK's controlled zone of international airspace. Moni-

Colorful Lufwaffe's 50 anniversary Eurofighter. [S. Mafé]

toring this zone ensures the safe passage for all other aircraft, including civilian transatlantic airliners that are under UK civilian air traffic control.

RAF air traffic controllers work at the UK National Air Traffic Service centre at Swanwick alongside their civilian counterparts to assist decision making.

The Russian aircraft were monitored throughout their flight by the National Air and Space Operations Centre at RAF High Wycombe and Air Surveillance and Control System at RAF Boulmer. Activity was coordinated closely with NATO allies, including the NATO Combined Air Operations Centre at Uedem in Germany.

A RAF Voyager tanker aircraft from RAF Brize Norton was also launched to provide air-to-air refuelling for the Typhoons.

Air Vice Marshal Duguid, Air Officer Commanding 11 Group said:

"The interception by RAF Typhoons and other NATO fighters of the Russian bombers for the third time in a week demonstrates our continuing resolve to police, protect and defend our airspace 24 hours a day, 365 days a year."

The RAF also provides deployed QRA support to NATO when needed and have previously operated from Estonia and Romania. Later this year, Typhoons from Lossiemouth will deploy to Lithuania in support of NATO air policing missions.

The badge of TakLwG 74. [S. Mafé]

Advanced Eurofighter Typhoons

Germany – luftwaffe

Project Quadriga

The German government is to replace its entire fleet of Tranche 1 Eurofighter combat aircraft under a new project revealed by Airbus Defence and Space (DS) on 5 November.

Speaking at the company's Manching facility near Munich, Kurt Rossner, Head of Air Combat, said that Airbus DS is close to signing a contract with Berlin to replace the Luftwaffe's 38 Tranche 1 Eurofighters under a programme to be called Project Quadriga. These early aircraft would then be sold to the international market before being replaced in Luftwaffe service by new-build Tranche 3 platforms that will include the E-Scan Mk 1 active electronically scanned array (AESA) radar and updated software.

"I would say that we are within weeks of signing the Quadriga contract with the German government - we are now in the final stages," Rossner said, adding that the sale of these early-variant aircraft will deliver the necessary capacity for the Luftwaffe as it looks to replace them with the latest-standard models. The 38 aircraft comprise seven twin-seaters and 26 single-seaters, with options for a further five single-seaters. No customer has yet been secured for these Tranche 1 aircraft to be sold-off.

The German government is to replace its entire fleet of Tranche 1 Eurofighter combat aircraft under a new project revealed by Airbus Defence and Space (DS) on 5 November.
Speaking at the company's Manching facility near Munich, Kurt Rossner, Head of Air Combat, said that Airbus DS is close to signing a contract with Berlin to replace the Luftwaffe's 38 Tranche 1 Eurofighters under a programme to be called Project Quadriga. Initial Eurofighter ECR capability is expected to be available by 2026, followed by further development steps and full integration into the future combat air system (FCAS) ecosystems. [Eurofighter]

While the Quadriga-standard Eurofighter is geared at the Luftwaffe, Rossner said that Switzerland would be a good match also as it looks to replace its ageing Northrop F-5E/F Tiger II and Boeing F/A-18 Hornet fleets. Airbus has proposed up to 40 Eurofighters for Switzerland, with type selection by the Federal Council due at the end of 2020 / early 2021.

Eurofighter ECR

Collaborative electronic warfare capabilities are essential for future combined air operations.

Initial Eurofighter ECR capability is expected to be available by 2026, followed by further development steps and full integration into the future combat air system (FCAS) ecosystems.

Eurofighter ECR will be able to provide passive emitter location as well as active jamming of threats, and will offer a variety of modular configurations for electronic attack (EA) and

Eurofighter has offered Finland the chance to join Europe's largest combat aircraft programme in an updated proposal to the HX fighter acquisition programme. The proposal has been submitted by the UK Government with the support of the Governments of Germany, Italy and Spain, the nations which are represented in the Eurofighter industry consortium. [MoD/RAF]

suppression/destruction of enemy air defence (SEAD/DEAD). Latest national escort jammer technology will ensure national control over features such as mission data and data analysis. The concept also features a new twin-seat cockpit configuration with a multi-function panoramic touch display and a dedicated mission cockpit for the rear-seat.

The concept is driven by the leading aerospace companies Airbus, Hensoldt, MBDA, MTU, Premium Aerotec, Rolls-Royce and supported by the German national industry bodies BDSV and BDLI. It specifically targets the German Air Force requirements for an airborne electronic attack capability. Furthermore it is the single opportunity to deliver such capabilities on the basis of national sovereignty, whilst also securing key military technologies within Germany.

Eurofighter is the backbone of German air defence. With more than 600 aircraft under contract and a workforce of 100.000 it is the largest collaborative defence programme in Europe to date.

Airbus Defence and Space (DS) has showcased a new electronic attack and counter-ground-based air defence variant of the Eurofighter combat aircraft as it looks to secure Germany's Tornado replacement requirement.

Speaking at the company's Manching facility in southern Germany on 5 November, Kurt Rossner, head of Air Combat, provided the first insight into Airbus DS plans for an Electronic Combat Reconnaissance (ECR)/ Suppression of Enemy Air Defences (SEAD) version of the Eurofighter to replace the Luftwaffe's Tornado ECR aircraft. This Tornado ECR replacement covers 40 aircraft as part of the wider Tornado IDR/ECR replacement programme for 85 aircraft.

As noted by Rossner, the ECR/SEAD configuration is a collaborative German industrial effort and forms part of the key technology roadmap for the aircraft. An ECR/SEAD Eurofighter offers the possibility of combining the escort and stand-in jammer platforms of any strike package, with an initial capability to be gained through podded systems before a more integrated solution is developed.

The ECR/SEAD configuration shown by Airbus comprises a pair of escort jammer pods on the underwing stations currently typically used to carry drop tanks, while three 1,000 litre tanks would be carried on the centreline and two inboard underwing pylons. These three stations are currently 'dry', and would need to be plumbed to carry fuel tanks. The aircraft is also shown carrying the SPEAR-EW weapon recently showcased by MBDA as a future SEAD weapons system, wingtip emitter locator stations, and both short- and long-range air-to-air missiles.

As noted by Rossner, the ECR/SEAD Eurofighter would "almost certainly" be a twin-seat aircraft with the rear cockpit devoted to operating the complex mission systems.

The ECR/SEAD configuration is part of a wider long-term capability development plan for the Typhoon combat aircraft that will span the coming decades.

Announced at the Paris Airshow in June, this project that has been agreed with the NATO Eurofighter and Tornado Management Agency (NETMA) on behalf of the partner countries, is called the Long-Term Evolution (LTE) plan.

Finland

Eurofighter submits updated proposal to HX programme

Eurofighter has offered Finland the chance to join Europe's largest combat aircraft programme in an updated proposal to the HX fighter acquisition programme.

The proposal has been submitted by the UK Government with the support of the Governments of Germany, Italy and Spain, the nations which are represented in the Eurofighter industry consortium.

It offers Finland sovereign control of its defence capability and security of supply as well as a combat proven, swing-role aircraft which will form the backbone of European defence for decades to come.

The detailed proposal updates on the original offer made to the HX fighter acquisition programme to replace the Finnish Air Force's F-18 Hornet aircraft.

John Rossall, Campaign Director at BAE Systems which is working alongside the UK Government on the offer to Finland, said:

We are delighted to present our updated proposal to Finland on behalf of the Eurofighter consortium.

Our proposal is an invitation to Finland to join leading nations in Europe with a shared defence objective.

By choosing Eurofighter, the Finnish Air Force would not only be acquiring the most advanced, multi-role aircraft on the market, it would be choosing everything Finland needs to operate, maintain and control its own aircraft in peacetime and in times of crisis.

In January, Eurofighter took part in the HX Challenge Flight Evaluation Trials, led by the Finnish Defence Forces in Tampere.

The trials saw two Royal Air Force jets perform over a five-day period to demonstrate many of the capabilities which form the offering of the Eurofighter consortium, which teams BAE Systems alongside leading European defence contractors Airbus and Leonardo.

Ahead of the trials, representatives of the Governments of the UK, Germany, Italy and Spain confirmed their commitment to a capability roadmap which will keep Eurofighter in the frontline of European defence for decades to come, the Long Term Evolution.

If you ever wondered about the typical kind of equipment that's required for a Typhoon to work efficiently, then our colleagues from the German Air Force have come up with an eye-catching answer! During the multinational fighter exercise Blue Flag 2019 in Israel they took time out to contribute to the latest viral trend called the Tetris Challenge. The Pilot and Maintenance team participated in the challenge, which involves emergency and military forces around the world. The pictures produced offer a rare glimpse of the equipment used by all the participating servicemen. [Bundeswehr/Jane Schmidt]

Spain – Ejército del aire

The retrofit of Tranche 1, the integration of the E-Scan radar and a possible replacement of the Spanish fleet of 85 F-18 aircraft are the most important pillars for the future of the jet-fighter in Spain.

On 19 February 2020, the Spanish Air Force received its last Eurofighter jet (C-16-78/14-36), reaching the 73 deliveries agreed in the original contract, Airbus DS sources told ESD during a visit to the company's facilities in Getafe, near Madrid.

However, this milestone does not spell the end for Spain's Eurofighter Ttyphoon programme as the Spanish Air Force (Ejército del Aire) will enhance its current fleet of 70 aircraft (there were three accidents in 2014, 2017 and 2018) and, most importantly, will replace 85 F-18 HORNET by 2025.

"The Eurofighter is a solid candidate for the replacement of the F-18 deployed in Zaragoza, Madrid and Canary Islands", a Spanish Air Force spokesperson said. The final decision is also linked to the possibility of reinforcing the industrial capabilities of Airbus DS in Spain. Of course, there are two other US-made candidates, the F-18Super Hornet by Boeing and F-35 Lightning II by Lockheed Martin.

Anyway, the Spanish government changed its defence staff members in after the last general election was won by the current socialist government. According to political analysts, the of Defence, Secretary of State, and part of the Chiefs of the Armed Forces could be replaced and a new team would have to make the final decision about the F-18 replacement.

However, on 14 December 2018, the current minister, Margarita Robles, approved an extra €906M to improve the capabilities of the Eurofighter fleet until 2023 "since the €9,254M of the allocated budget had been spent."

Official Airbus sources have expressed their satisfaction with the statements of the Spanish MoD, which spell out Spain's plans for the future of its Eurofighter fleet: "We hope to work with this valuable client to implement the proposed improvements that will ensure the fundamental role of Eurofighter at the heart of the Spanish Air Force during the next decades and that will underpin the continuous stability of the production of combat aircraft in Spain."

On the 23rd December 2019 at the Flight Test Centre of Leonardo Aircraft Division in Turin-Caselle, the first Instrumented Series Production Aircraft (ISPA 6) equipped with the Kuwait Air Force configuration has successfully completed its first flight.
The aircraft is the first to fly the innovative Captor E-Scan Radar with Phase Enhancement P3Eb, and is a key milestone for the entry into service of Eurofighter with the State of Kuwait.
This standard is the most advanced variant of the fighter jet ever made, with a package of capabilities that builds effectively on existing enhancement programmes.
A contract for the supply of 28 Eurofighter Typhoon multi-role fighter aircraft was signed between the Ministry of Defence of the State of Kuwait and Leonardo (on 05 April 2016) through its Aircraft Division acting as Eurofighter Prime Contractor Organisation.
With Captor E-Scan radar and several new additions to the weapon system, this variant will put the Kuwait Air Force at the front-line of the fighter technology when the aircraft will enter into service with the State of Kuwait in 2020.
While other aircraft in different Eurofighter Partner Companies are testing specific parts of this configuration, including the development of the E-Scan radar in UK and Germany, this is the first flight of the entire package that will be delivered to Kuwait.
The capability package for Kuwait includes the integration of Storm Shadow and Brimstone and other air-to-surface weapons. Moreover it foresees the integration of a new advanced laser designator pod (the Lockheed Martin Sniper Advanced Targeting Pod) that will expand Eurofighter's portfolio of cleared laser designator pods; the introduction of the DRS-Cubic ACMI P5 combat training pod and an enhanced navigation aid (VOR). [Eurofighter]

Spain participates in the Eurofighter programme by holding 14% of Airbus DS (Germany with Airbus DS, 30%; UK with BAE Systems, 36%; Italy with Leonardo, 20%). The final assembly line in Getafe provides the delivery of the entire Spanish Eurofighter fleet and manufactures all the right-hand wing of all 623 aircrafts ordered by nine countries (Germany, UK, Italy, Spain, Austria, Saudi Arabia, Kuwait, Oman and Qatar).

The Tranche 1 Retrofit

"The replacement of Tranche 1 EUROFIGHTER is not an issue at the moment. Tranche 1 fleet has just started a modernisation programme, which includes hardware and software upgrades, taking care of obsolescence issues by integrating Tranche 2 hardware. Operational upgrades include new capabilities, like the possibility of carry Litening targeting pods" (in fact the new Litening Vs have been purchased to supplement the earlier Litening III), the official spokesperson of the Spanish Air Force, Lieutenant-Colonel Marcos Díez Estévez, told us.

In february 2019, Airbus delivered the first upgraded Tranche 1 EUROFIGHTER to the Spanish Air Force. The upgrade was carried out at the Airbus facilities in Getafe and involved the introduction of hardware modifications, which support the Operational Flight Programme 02 (OFP-02) developed by the Armament and Experimental Logistics Centre (CLAEX) in the Spanish Air Force.

The upgrade developed by Airbus includes modifications that integrate Tranche 2 and Tranche 3 equipment on the aircraft, such as a Computer Symbol Generator, Digital Video and Voice Recorder, Laser Designator Pod and Maintenance Data Panel.

The last if the inicial order of Eurofighter Typhoons for the Spanish Air Force, serialled C.14-78/14-36 left the Airbus Defence and Space assembly line at Getafe, Madrid, Spain on January 2020, sproting this colorful vertical fin assembly, with the words "Volando Hacia el Futuro" (Flying into the Future). [EdA]

"This first single-seat Eurofighter (serial number SS003), to be followed by a second two-seat aircraft currently undergoing the upgrade, will be used initially by CLAEX as a test aircraft for the qualification of these new capabilities that will be implemented on the Air Force's fleet of 17 Tranche 1 Eurofighters", Fernando Peces, responsible for the EUROFIGHTER programme at Airbus DS in Spain, stated.

Another pillar of the Phase 2 Enhancements (P2E) of the Spanish Eurofighter will be the integration of the METEOR missile. Developed and produced by a consortium of European companies led by MBDA, the METEOR missile is undoubtedly the main innovation of the P2E.

On 19 February 2020, this jet was handed over to the Spanish Air Force's Ala 14 at Los Llanos-Albacete air base, being flown from Getafe by Captain Fernando "Nando" Caballero de Pro, that th especial painting on the fin has been removed. [EdA]

Ala 14 personnel posing in fron of C.16-78, Captain Caballero is ninth from the left. [EdA]

METEOR is a radar missile designed to destroy targets at previously unattainable distances. Its maximum range is well over 100 kilometres, twice as long as other missiles designed for combat beyond the visual line of sight (BVLoS), including the US AMRAAM, which remains the most important reference to date.

Being a fully European technology, METEOR contributes to the autonomy of the continent in terms of defence with a truly revolutionary product, which has no equivalent in the market. In addition to the Eurofighter, this missile has been integrated into the Swedish Gripen, the French Rafale and the British F-35.

E-Scan Integration

After the retrofit of Tranche 1 in 2023, Airbus DS wants to introduce E-Scan radar in the entire fleet. This adaptation will imply improvements in the following capacities: detection, attack and identification; SAR modes (synthetic aperture radar); transmission of images; electromagnetic measurements; and integration of smart weapons.

The integration of the E-Scan radar is a binational programme involving Spain and Germany to start in 2022 in the Luftwaffe. It will bring about an improvement in the processing and electronic warfare functions, the radar is known as Mk., initially the 19 surviving Ala 14 Tranche 3A will receive the new radar in the period 2024-2025.

And the F-18 Spanish Fleet Replacement?

What are the possibilities for EUROFIGHTER to replace the 85 F-18 HORNETs fleet of the Spanish Air Force? After the integration of the

The integration of the E-Scan radar is a bi-national programme involving Spain and Germany to start in 2022 in the Luftwaffe. It will bring about an improvement in the processing and electronic warfare functions, the radar is known as Mk., initially the 19 surviving Ala 14 Tranche 3A will receive the new radar in the period 2024-2025. [Euroradar]

E-Scan radar into the current fleet, Airbus DS expects to win a new contract to replace the F-18s.

"We are having conversations with the Spanish MoD to replace the F-18. Of course, it is a sovereign decision. But, I can tell you that the favourite option to replace the first F-18 aircraft in Gando Air Base (Canary Islands) is the Eurofighter", Alberto Gutiérrez, head of military aircraft at Airbus DS, told ESD. This is where a new chapter in the 'jet flight' between Europe and US is about to begin.

In fact the prediction is that 20 Eurofighter Typhoon Tranche 4, Block 60 will replace the 462 Escuadrón (Ala 46) F/A-18A Hornets, based at Gando airfield, Gran Canaria, during the period 2024-2027, as said before, and these will be delivered five jets per year, in the so-called "Proyecto Halcón" (Project Hawk). Those Typhoons will be pre-LTE Long Term Evolution), the LTEs will have new hardware/software architecture, including a wide area touchscreem instrument panel. Hopefully, the Spanish AF intends to pruchase 40 of these to replace Ala 15 F-18M Hornets from 2030-2032, and possibly Ala 12 (the other F-18M user will be equipped with F-35A Lighting II.

Eurofighter enhancement

Eurofighter Jagdflugzeug GmbH and NETMA, the NATO Eurofighter & Tornado Management Agency, have signed a contract worth close to €300 million for the Consolidation Package

A Spanish Tranche 2 belonging to Ala 11 at Morón. [S. Mafé]

Just after take-off, the landing gear starts its retraction sequence. [S. Mafé]

This vew of "11-53", clearly shows the Typhoon's delta wing platform. [EdA]

Step Two & Three – Phase 1 Contract. It provides the next steps in the capability evolution of the Eurofighter Typhoon combat aircraft. Here we explain what it involves.

What does this contract facilitate?

It's essentially a suite of contracts which provides the next step of Typhoon capability enhancements for Eurofighter's core and export customers. It consolidates different streams into one product to form a firm baseline for onwards capability evolution.

An important element of the contract deals with capability enhancements for operating Typhoon with the Meteor beyond visual range, air-to-air missile, with the capability implementation being transferred from the M-Scan to E-Scan radar.

It also includes improvements to the way Typhoon operates with the Brimstone precision air-to-surface capability; adaptations to the cockpit display formats; enhancements to interoperability through MIDS Link 16 and radio; and improvements to the defensive aids sub system (DASS).

It's a comprehensive set of individual capabilities, mostly in the avionics domain, but also some extensions to the air vehicle clearance envelopes. As such, its development utilises

Section take-off of a Typhoon pair belonging to Ala 14. [EdA]

skills from across the engineering and support spectrum. It is the natural continuation of the drumbeat of consistent capability releases for Eurofighter customers.

What is the value of the contract?

The initial first phase of the contract is just under the 300 million euros, with a planned amendment to introduce additional capabilities, (e.g. regulatory compliance). After the initial phase of the contract a second phase, scheduled for award in mid-2022, will provide coverage through to completion.

What will the capabilities bring for Eurofighter customers?

The Consolidation Package represents an evolution of the capabilities of the aircraft. Taken together this package makes the weapon system better and more versatile for end user air forces, with improvements to individual capabilities being rolled out across the whole fleet of M-Scan and E-Scan aircraft.

Through updates to Typhoon's operational capability with Meteor and Brimstone, the contract strengthens both the air-to-air and air-to-surface capabilities of the weapon system and rolls these updates out across the whole fleet.

At the same time, it significantly improves the platform's interoperability with coalition forces through the enhancements to the MIDS and radios. The changes to cockpit display formats follow on from feedback from the operator community who have asked for certain changes to improve the pilot and machine interaction.

Where will the work take place?

The activity will primarily take place within the four Eurofighter industry partners — BAE Systems, Airbus Germany, Airbus Spain and Leonardo — but with significant aspects being undertaken within the wider supply base, most specifically EuroRadar and EuroDASS.

Why is having a harmonised product so important?

It is important to optimise our efforts because it is a more efficient way of developing capability. Making the product common, still allowing customisations but keeping the core of the product joint. This helps to simplify the product landscape and drives efficiency into the development process.

Who has been involved in pulling the work together?

The project teams in Eurofighter and the Eurofighter industry partners — in engineering, commercial, programmes, finance and support — have worked together through the bid process.

The programme launched with industry prefunding because the industry partners recognised the importance of this work. Industry has undertaken significant engineering activities that not only made the contract award possible, but also recognised the delivery timescales required by our customers.

Overall, the approach has required commitment, innovation, transparency and collaboration across Europe, NETMA and the nations. We've overcome any challenges together.

A pair of Typhoons photographed from the rear ramp of an A400M. [M. Acosta]

The Quadriga deal is a long-term boost for Eurofighter.

Eurofighter Typhoon is confirmed as Germany's weapons system of choice, says Airbus' Head of Combat Aircraft Systems Kurt Rossner, following the country's decision to replace its existing Tranche 1 aircraft under the Quadriga programme.

"It's a really powerful message from a core customer," says Kurt, who is also Chairman of the Eurofighter Supervisory Board. "It's a sign of their appreciation of our performance. It says they are very happy with the aircraft because they could have postponed the order or even selected a different one."

He believes the deal, which extends the usage life of the Typhoon, will reinvigorate Europe's industrial defence base, boost the Eurofighter's export campaigns in Switzerland, Finland. Furthermore, the deal serves as a catalyst for future capability.

Under the deal, announced in the Bundestag in November, Germany has committed to 38 new Eurofighter Typhoon aircraft for the Luftwaffe. The aircraft will be built to the latest standard and include the E-Scan radar Mk1.

This news is a further boost for the Eurofighter programme, following the E-Scan radar retro-embodiment contracts for the Spanish Ejército del Aire and German Luftwaffe Typhoon fleets and the continuation of the development of E-Scan version Mk2 announced in the summer.

Kurt says that because Quadriga is a show of faith from one of the original core partners, the decision will resonate far and wide. It represents both a continuation in the production and, at the same time, a positive signal that the capability roadmap will be extended, because Germany is now committed to Eurofighter until at least 2050 – 2060.

The German Air Force is a very stable ecosystem, and, through Quadriga, it is clearly planning on the aircraft having an in-service life of at least 30 to 40 years.

"That means we have to enable Eurofighter's capability growth to meet their expectation. We look forward to further developing the aircraft to meet the future needs of the German Air Force, in terms of their mission requirements and the threat environment they will face. "Clearly Eurofighter will be an essential part of the future combat [FCAS] ecosystem and play a part in the system of systems. That means we have to grow the aircraft capability to meet the demands of the FCAS environment."

The industrial impact

Ahead of the Quadriga signing, the Eurofighter Partner Companies (EPCs), Airbus Germany, Airbus Spain, BAE Systems and Leonardo, worked together on a plan to bridge the production gap following the completion of the final Tranche 3 jet.

At the Airbus facility in Manching, Germany, Quadriga started life in 2020 with about

100 people working on the long-term initiative, the planning, preparation and procurement elements. When the first major components arrive for equipping the team will grow to almost 200 to 250.

By 2023 Airbus will start preparing the final assembly again and will grow the team further. In total there will be around 150 to 200 people out of the Manching Eurofighter workforce up to 3000 working purely on Quadriga tasks.

However, Kurt says that this is not simply a job numbers story. "That's a quantitative issue, the qualitative issue is more important. People are extremely proud to work on this programme and to work on a new aircraft.

"Currently Manching is carrying out excellent work delivering centre fuselages for export to Qatar and Kuwait. But we really miss having brand new aircraft to deliver. It's a different mindset. It fills you with pride and because of that Quadriga is a real boost for the site."

Though work on the final assembly will start in 2023, the production process is already underway starting with procuring the titanium and other metals required. "We have a very detailed plan for each of the aircraft. All the industry partners started their long-term activities even before the deal was signed because we did not want to have a production gap after the Kuwait and Qatar aircraft are completed. We have already embedded our plans into a production continuation plan."

Export boost

Kurt says the fact that Germany has decided to back Eurofighter once again is a strong sales message. "If you have a fully convinced, happy customer procuring the same product, that demonstrates they are happy with the performance, with the support, with everything. It's just like if you buy the same car for the second time — it speaks volumes about how happy you are with that model.

For Eurofighter this is a huge demonstration of support, even better than an export customer win in some respects, because it's a continuation and thus a very positive signal.

This is a programme that is very much alive. The contract sends a strong message to potential export countries like Finland, Switzerland, Egypt and Bangladesh that they can be assured that this aircraft will be in service up to 2060.

It says there is a fully committed partner there for long-term partnerships. In terms of export opportunities, I believe the contract is a huge enabler.

Covid pressures

The Eurofighter chairman says that the consortium partners have been working closely together over the past 12 months, and he puts that down to a number of factors but in 2020 one stands out: Covid-19. "A crisis tests you and really shows if you can work together. I think the community passed that test, came much closer together and is now much stronger."

But, he says, there's a looming challenge. The response to the pandemic has hit Europe

These to Spanish Typhoons carry the Litening III pod on the centerline station. [M. Acosta]

Ala 14 has on strengh two Eurofighter Typhoon Ts (two-seaters). [EdA]

hard and forced governments into big unforeseen spending commitments in order to support their domestic economies and health services.

"The big risk we face is budgets. The pressure on defence budgets will inevitably be higher because of Covid and therefore the relationships between industry must be better. Programme performance and affordability will have to improve, and this can only happen if the four EPCs work even closer together, defining their values and their targets together.

We are all very willing to do this and work hand-in-hand as one team – industry and nations."

In March 2020 there was an agreement between the whole Eurofighter Enterprise around the 10-year plan for the programme. This, says Kurt, is a key enabler for the future joint working. "The plan is a baseline for planning and understanding. It is a common plan — not an industry plan, not a core nation plan but a common plan, with common goals and a shared roadmap for us to go on. It is important because it will help us in terms of affordability and speed."

While budgets will inevitably come under pressure, Kurt says Eurofighter will be able to make a strong argument for investment in terms of skills and IP. He says a programme like Eurofighter ensures the technical knowledge base in the respective core nations is sustained.

"The knowledge we have gained over the decades in the different nations can be sustained with the continuation of production contracts and with the development of capability enhancements and the Long Term Evolution [LTE]."

Evolution story

Kurt says a further challenge for Eurofighter industry partners will be to demonstrate to customer nations, both export and core nations, that they can deliver new capability more expediently. "We need to develop capability in faster and shorter cycles.

We currently have a two-year cycle but in the future, we need to deliver a full capability enhancement package over a 12-month cycle."

A key area will be computing power and the avionics as new software architecture will have to be adopted. "We need to improve the software architecture into a more easily handled software configuration. We also need to be ready to adopt different missions.

"The UK, thorough Project Centurion, did a good job of transferring their Tornado missions onto the aircraft. Now we need to be prepared for the same thing in Germany because the next big opportunity will be the Tornado replacement contract. We need to be able to transfer Tornado missions onto the Eurofighter, which means additional weapons and additional capability.

In Germany we will also demonstrate that we can even further improve the excellent flight performance and stability of the aircraft to carry different weapons. This is called the Aerodynamic Modification Kit [AMK]. It's about generating even higher longitudinal stability of the aircraft's aerodynamics to new potential weapon integration.

Looking to the future battlespace, where the Quadriga standard aircraft will operate, Kurt

says Eurofighter will also play a role in helping de-risk technologies for next generation fighters too. "If you were to define and design a new aircraft like the Tempest or FCAS from scratch, there would be a high risk of failure in one area. But having a stable aircraft like Eurofighter means you can implement technology enhancement programmes without risk. Take communication, for example, you can develop communication capability to other assets in the system of systems and implement it on a stable platform like Eurofighter.

"You can gain from Eurofighter knowledge and transfer technology, which was proven on a stable platform, into the future combat aircraft system, Tempest or FCAS. For the engineers it's an excellent test bed, while at the same time Eurofighter capability improves ensuring its transfer into a new generation system environment."

Kurt says that in the short-term Eurofighter will be concentrating its efforts on the next potential customer: Spain. Eurofighter has submitted proposals for the replacement of the Spanish Air Force's F-18s which are based on the Canary

Close-up of an Añla 14 Eurofighter Typhoon, note the position of the canards. [EdA]

An Ala 11 Eurofighter landing at Gando air base, during the Ocean Sky Exercise, October 2021. [Manuel Acosta]

Line-up of Ala 14 Typhoons heading to runway 03R during Ocean Sky Exercise, October 2021. [Manuel Acosta]

Islands. Spain is looking to secure 20 new Eurofighter Typhoon aircraft to boost its existing fleet under what is called Project Halcon. Airbus is in the process of negotiations with the Spanish government to mature the proposal and a contract for the 20 aircraft is expected to be signed in 2021.

"Quadriga is proof to Spain of how it will work," he says. "We also want to provide industry with even longer sustainability on production by securing more export contracts with Switzerland and Finland.

For Germany the next big target will be to prepare the proposal for replacing the aligning fleet of Tornado by Eurofighter.

"And finally, to create a technology roadmap — the LTE plan. With the LTE agreement in place, we could deliver the Quadriga aircraft but enable them for additional retrofit programmes so that in 10, 15 years' time these aircraft are transformed into a much higher standard jet. We will be able to grow into the 2060s with this vision.

"The capability growth areas are more in terms of the missions, weapons and avionics, aero mod kit and these are all retrofittable. The good thing is we are starting from a point where the aircraft is already world class in terms of its baseline performance."

Acknowledgments

Many people and institutions have participated in the elaboration of this work, including Brigadier General Leon Antonio Machés Michavila, the Communication Office of the Air Force (Lieutenant Colonel Marcos Díez Estévez and Lieutenant Colonel José Manuel Bellido Laprada) to the Operations Group C.Os. of Ala 11 and Ala 14, Lieutenant Colonel Maximiliano García, Lieutenant Colonel Pascual Soria, to the General Secretariat of the Air Force of Albacete, to Jorge Portalés, Rafael Treviño (especially thank you very much, for his magnificent research work about the origins of the Eurofighter), Juanjo Fernández, Joaquín Sánchez, Jesús Pinillos, Miguel Moreno, Joaquín Ducay, Fernando Caballero, José María Martínez, Ignacio de los Pinos, Álvaro José Navia-Osorio, José Figueiredo, Pablo Gutiérrez, Ricardo Serrano, Juan Bengoechea, Goyo Arizaga, Ricardo Serrano, Tono Fernandez, Alberto Garrido, Geoff Lee and if I forget somebody, to all the staff of Group 11, Wing 14, MAESAL and CLAEX, their collaboration has been full; also to the AMI, RAF, Luftwaffe, NATO and the Austrian Air Force; also to Eurofighter Jagdflugzeug GMBH. and finally to my family for their unwavering support, especially to Mario, as this book is almost a job of both!

Eurofighter 2000 Typhoon

Drawings: Stanisław Krzysztof Mokwa

Sheet 1

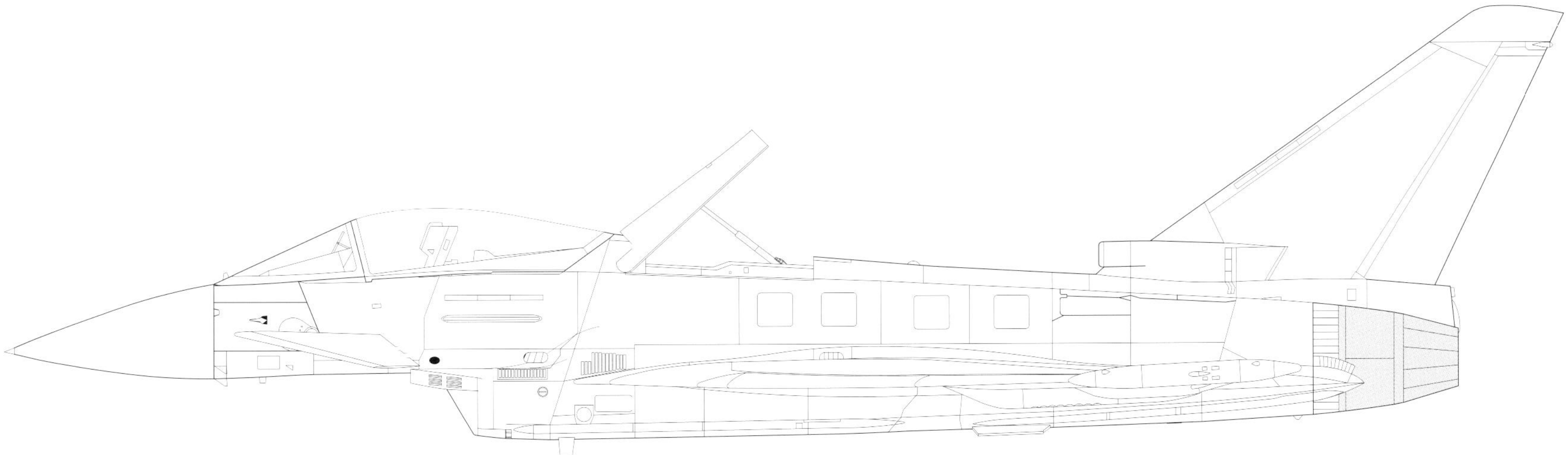

Eurofighter EF 2000 F

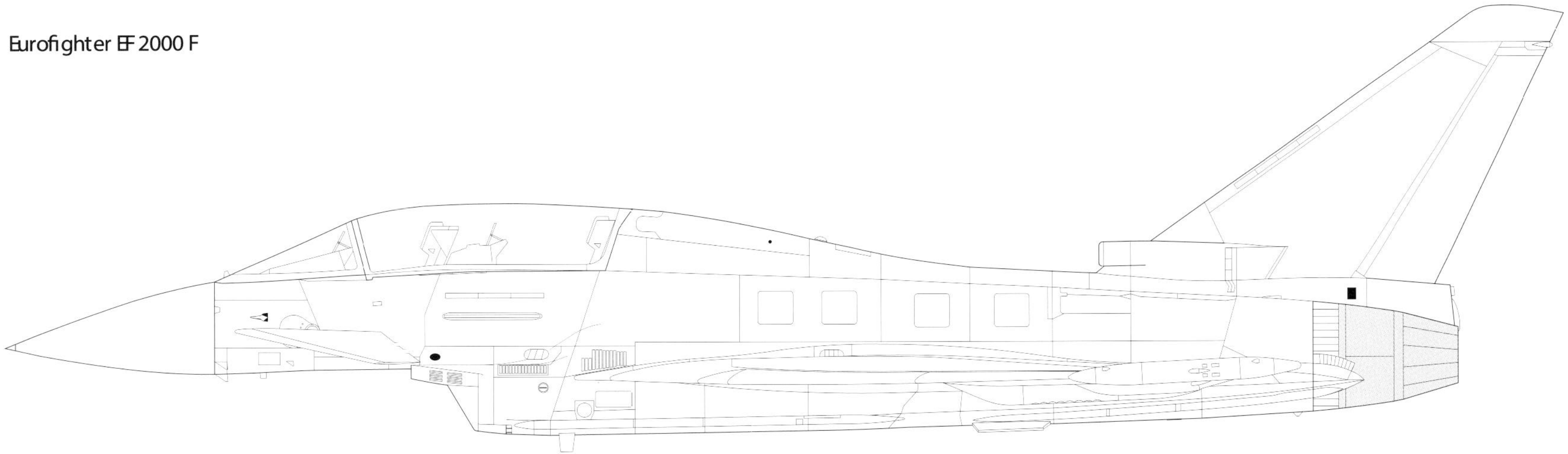

Eurofighter EF 2000 T (DA4)

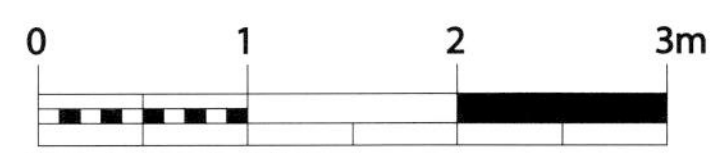

Sketch in scale 1/72

Eurofighter 2000 Typhoon

Drawings: Stanisław Krzysztof Mokwa

Sheet 2

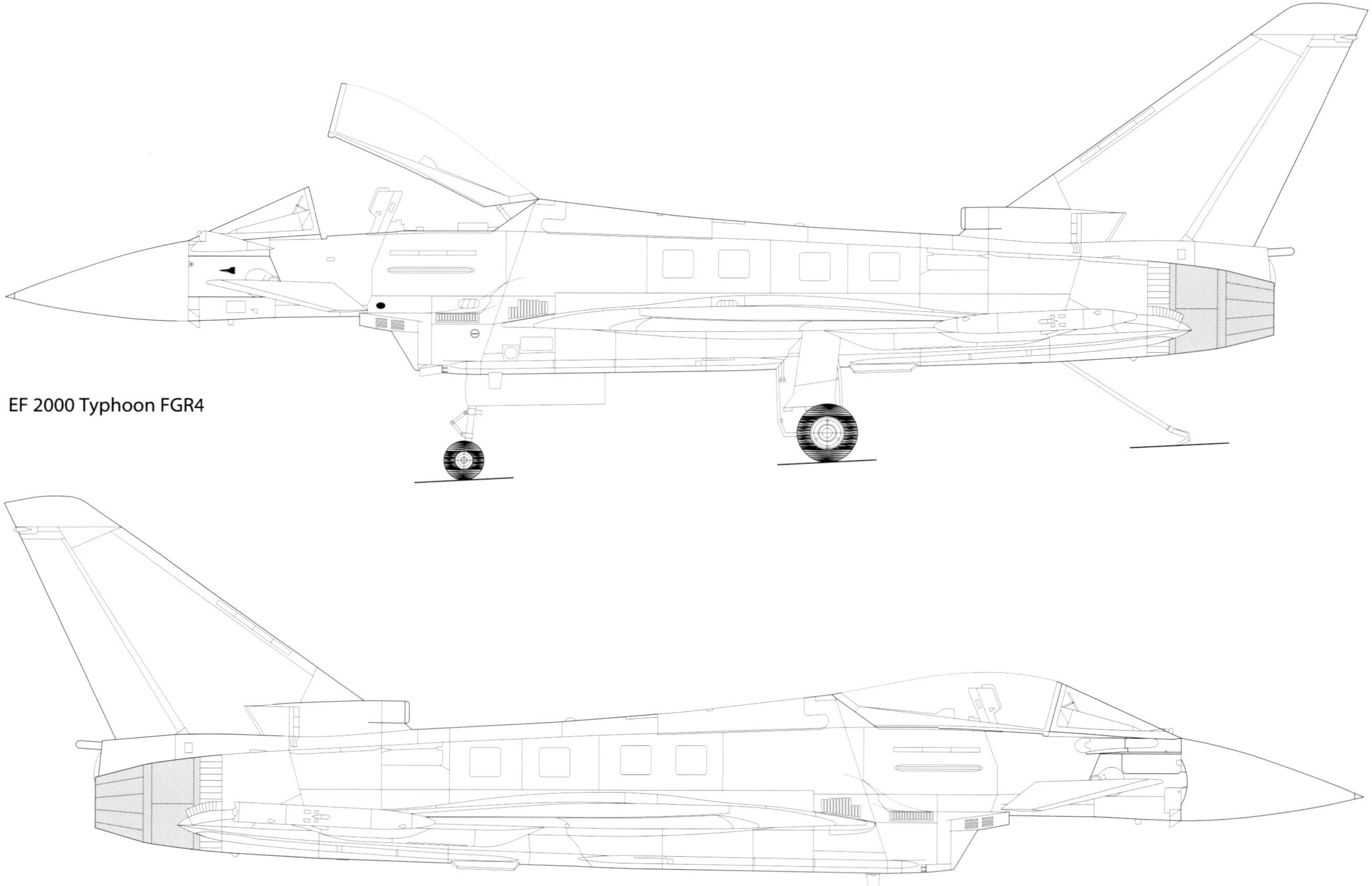

EF 2000 Typhoon FGR4

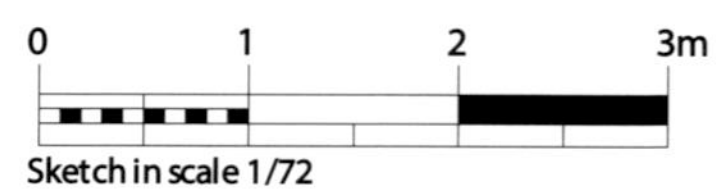

Eurofighter 2000 Typhoon

Drawings: Stanisław Krzysztof Mokwa

Sheet 3

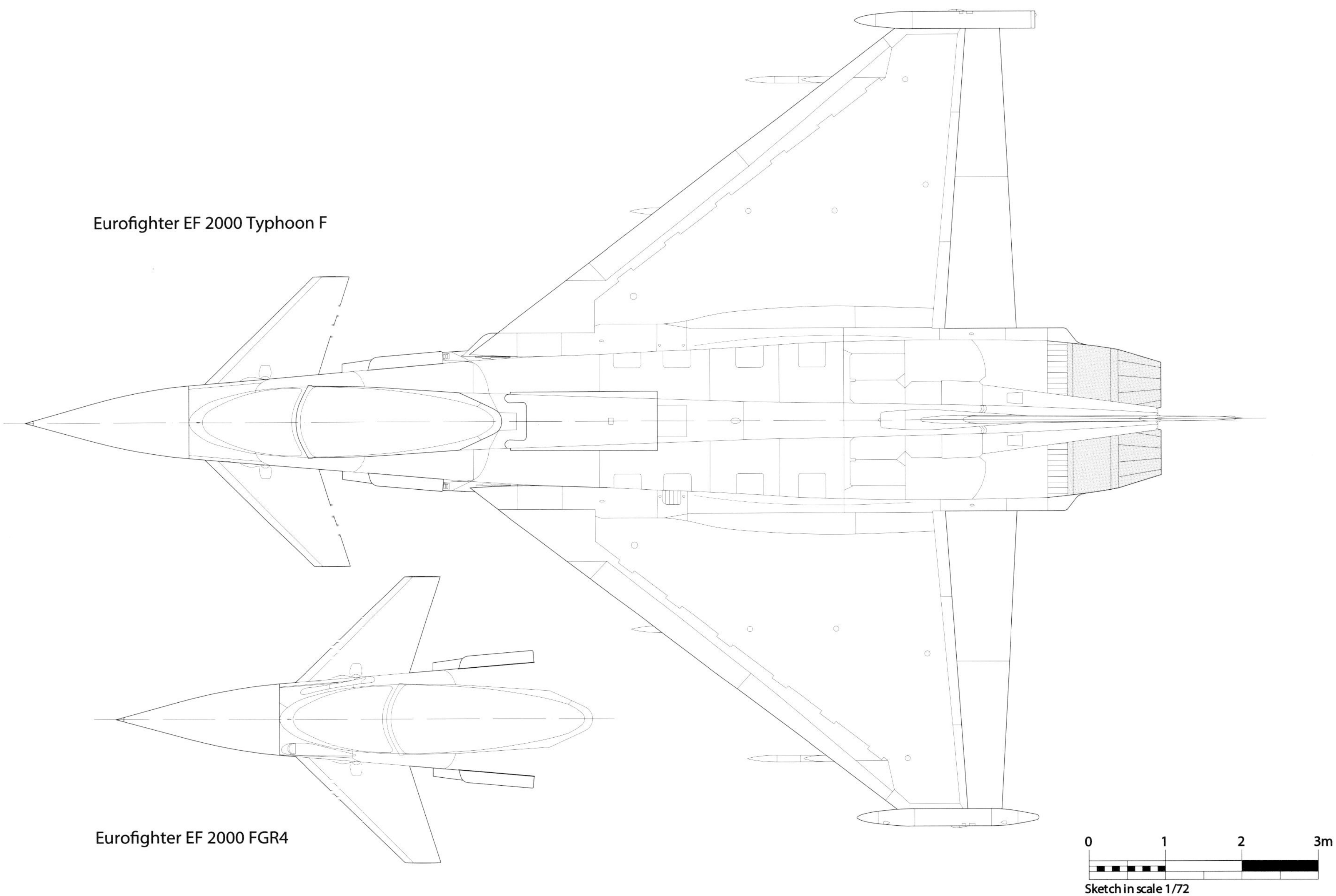

Eurofighter 2000 Typhoon

Drawings: Stanisław Krzysztof Mokwa

Sheet 4

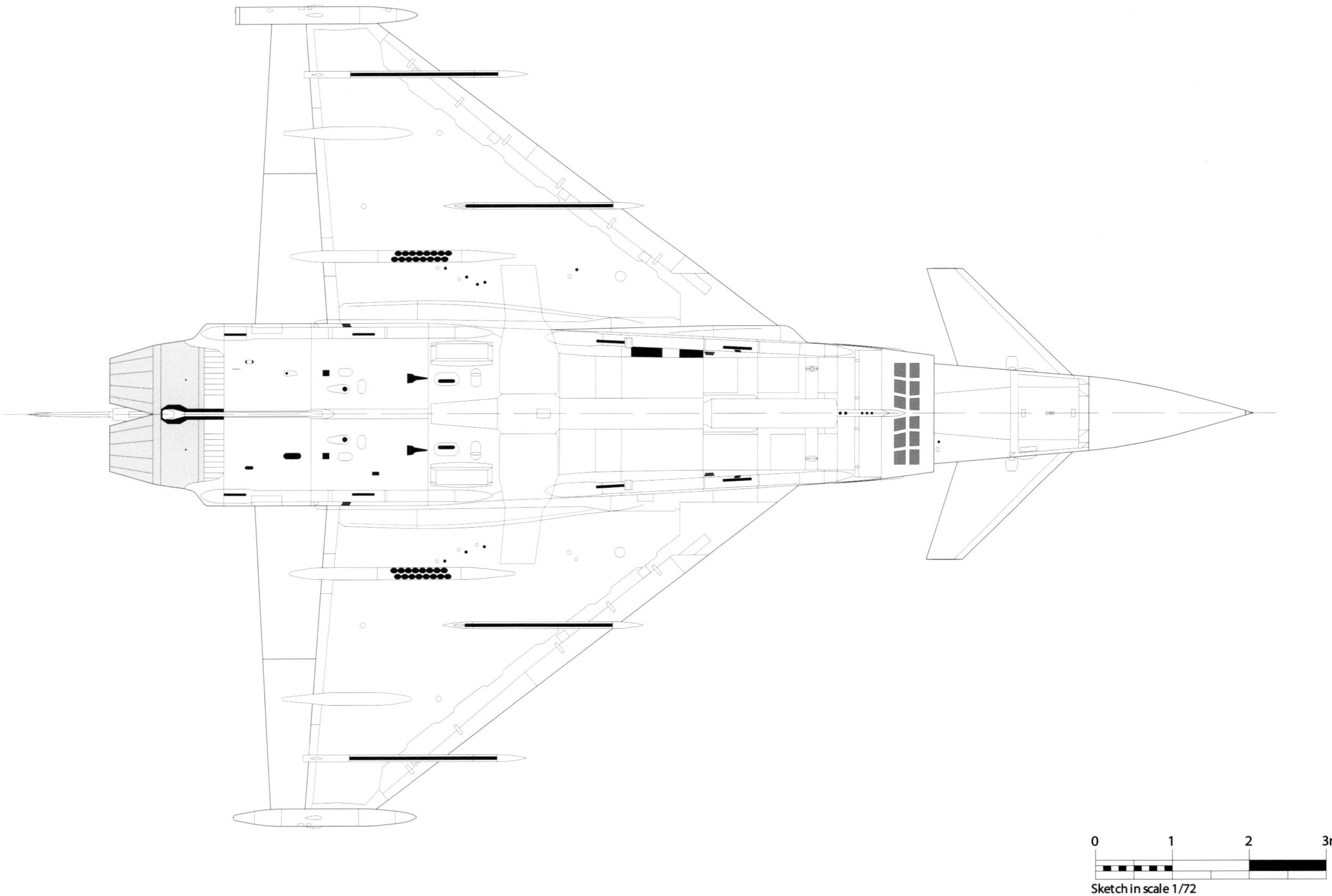